The New AYN RAND Companion

Revised and Expanded Edition

Mimi Reisel Gladstein

D0208306

GREENWOOD PRESS
Westport, Connecticut • London

Library of Congress Cataloging-in-Publication Data

Gladstein, Mimi Reisel.
    The new Ayn Rand companion / Mimi Reisel Gladstein. — Rev. and
expanded ed.
      p.   cm.
    Rev. ed. of: The Ayn Rand companion. 1984.
    Includes bibliographical references (p.   ) and index.
    ISBN 0–313–30321–5 (alk. paper)
    1. Rand, Ayn—Criticism and interpretation. 2. Women and
literature—United States—History—20th century. 3. Philosophy in
literature. 4. Objectivism (Philosophy) I. Gladstein, Mimi
Reisel. Ayn Rand companion. II. Title.
PS3535.A547Z67   1999
813'.52—dc21   98–50226

British Library Cataloguing in Publication Data is available.

Library of Congress Catalog Card Number: 98–50226
ISBN: 0–313–30321–5

First published in 1999

Greenwood Press, 88 Post Road West, Westport, CT 06881
An imprint of Greenwood Publishing Group, Inc.
www.greenwood.com

Printed in the United States of America

The paper used in this book complies with the
Permanent Paper Standard issued by the National
Information Standards Organization (Z39.48–1984).

10 9 8 7 6 5 4 3 2 1

The New Ayn Rand Companion
Revised and Expanded Edition

Ayn Rand in her academic gown for the presentation of a Doctor of Humane Letters (L.H.D.), Lewis and Clark College, October 2, 1963.

Once more to Jay
Still lightning and bedrock

Contents

Acknowledgments

For this revised edition, I am, of course, still beholden to all the people whose help and support contributed to the first edition of *The Ayn Rand Companion*. Thanks again to Arthur H. Stickney, John Hendley, Barbara Branden, Terry Diamond, Douglas Den Uyl, Nathaniel Branden, Helen and Jim Bell, Alice Gaspar de Alba, Larry Johnson, David Hall, Diana Natalicio, Monica Camarillo, and Vidal Oaxaca for their assistance in the original project.

Revising and updating *The New Ayn Rand Companion* has put me in debt to numerous others. Where the book accomplishes its purpose, I owe much to them. The faults and errors that remain are solely my own. Chief among those to whom I owe thanks is Chris Matthew Sciabarra. His generosity in sharing bibliographical information and responding to queries was exemplary. Equally important was the invaluable assistance of Peter Saint Andre, who, along with Chris, served as a first-line editor for this edition. Both made numerous editorial suggestions which strengthened the text. Thanks are also due to Michelle Marder Kamhi and Lou Torres for their helpful counsel. They reviewed the original *Companion* in order to recommend corrections and additions for this new edition. Matthew Stoloff was an important bibliographical resource. His contributions are much appreciated.

Over the years, readers of the original *Companion* have sent me supplementary information and materials, some of which I have included in this new edition. Rodney Schroeter contributed his expertise about the Ditko/Rand connection. Richard Shedenheim, Wayne Kline, and Gerry Sperry also sent materials. Thanks to Douglas Den Uyl and Tibor Machan for sharing advance copies of their forthcoming books, and to David Ramsay Steele for supplying an early copy of *The Ayn Rand Cult*.

Bob Poole and Scott McConnell provided helpful last minute biblio-graphical information.

Institutional support at the University of Texas at El Paso was pro-vided by Carl Jackson and Howard Daudistel in the form of reduced teaching loads and research support. Heather Smith was a helpful assis-tant. Special thanks to Rachel Murphree, reference librarian extraordi-naire. The bibliography would have been much reduced without her invaluable assistance. Much has happened in the field of Ayn Rand stud-ies in the more than dozen years since the first book was published, and search engines require a savvy genius, which she provided. Working again with Cynthia Harris, reminded me of how important an experi-enced editor is. Elizabeth Meagher provided invaluable production ed-iting and expeditious responses to my questions. Carol Blumentritt's painstaking attention to style and documentation detail helped improve the manuscript.

To Nathaniel Branden, a special note of thanks since it was his inquiry about the availability of the *Companion* that provided the impetus for this new edition.

If I leave anyone out to whom I owe my thanks, please understand it is not that I am not grateful, but at this moment my recollection has failed me. Thanking everyone who deserves one's thanks in the complex process of writing a book is a difficult task. The acknowledgment chapter is usually the last written and unfortunately memory sometimes fails just when we need it the most.

Finally, my gratitude, as always, to my husband Jay. Our partnership is the bedrock of my personal and professional fulfillment.

Introduction

The New Ayn Rand Companion introduces readers to the writings—fiction and nonfiction—of Ayn Rand (1905–1982). Rand was a Russian émigré who came to this country in 1926 and became one of the foremost proponents of capitalism. By the time she died, her name had become synonymous with rugged individualism and titanic self-assertion. She loved the United States and considered it the most moral country in history. Her great fear was that Americans were losing sight of the American way and succumbing to decadent European philosophies.

As a companion, this study is constructed to serve a variety of purposes. Its primary function is as a resource for both personal and academic research. A number of its initial readers found it not only useful for research but also pleasurable for its ability to recall for them clear images of many of the Rand characters and theories they had enjoyed in the past. *The New Companion* is designed to appeal to sundry audiences: (1) Readers who have read Rand and are intrigued to know more about the author and her works; (2) Students of philosophy who may have been introduced to Objectivism and would like to find out where they can learn more about it and its originator; (3) Researchers who are interested in both overview and bibliography; (4) People interested in contemporary culture; (5) The general reader whose interest in Rand was piqued for whatever reason. Rand is a unique personality and the study of her works provides satisfaction for diverse appetites.

The above truth was illustrated for me repeatedly as I worked on this book. Interest in Rand was ubiquitous. Our local newspaper published a review I had written about the latest study of John Steinbeck; I received a number of calls as a result of that review, but none of them were from people interested in Steinbeck. The calls were inspired by the short biographical note that indicated that I was working on a book on Ayn

Rand. The calls were not from contemporaries, but from young people with diverse backgrounds: a swimming coach, a philosophy student, a lawyer, a libertarian activist. They were all hungry for the opportunity to discuss Rand and her works and were pleased to find that they were not alone in their interest. Never, in all my years of reviewing for our local newspapers, have I had strangers call me in response to a review. What struck me as particularly significant was that most of them had not been born when Rand's last novel, *Atlas Shrugged*, was published. A chance remark, in a social setting, that I was writing about Rand brought unsolicited testimonies from casual acquaintances affirming the strong influence she had had on their lives. All this in El Paso, Texas, where her philosophy was never taught.

Her name was universally mispronounced. When I said I was writing about Ayn (which is pronounced to rhyme with *mine* or *pine*) Rand, most people said, "Oh yes, Anne Rand." Or they pronounced the name Ayn as if it rhymed with *main*. However, rare was the individual who did not know who she was, once we agreed on pronunciation.

Writing about Rand has pitfalls unlike those attendant to most critical endeavors. Rand's theories do not provoke ambivalent responses. If she is not held in awe, she is usually despised. One's academic peers, whose politics are generally left of center, consider her political theories a little to the right of the far-right-wing John Birch Society, and they question the wisdom of your choice of subjects. These same individuals would not question the study of Ezra Pound, who was a rabid anti-Semite and made treasonous broadcasts in the service of Fascist governments. So much for academic objectivity.

If Rand's antagonists are suspicious of anyone who is writing about her, Rand and her acknowledged followers are doubly wary. Rand has been attacked so often and so viciously that they are concerned that she be represented fairly. Rand questioned the motives of anyone who was not within the pale. She was particularly watchful that her theories not be appropriated to advance causes she was not in agreement with. Another of her concerns was that her ideas, which she considered her property, not be exploited to the financial benefit of someone else. She was given to litigiousness.[1] She sued a publisher for using her name in the promotional material for a book.[2] While Rand encouraged students, supporters, and friends to study, discuss, and disseminate Objectivist ideas, she warned against those who would attempt to act as "spokesmen for Objectivism."[3]

My purpose in this work is to present as unbiased an overview of the Ayn Rand oeuvre as possible; my goal is to contribute to research resources rather than engage in polemics. However, because of the pitfalls already mentioned, I think I should clarify my position vis à vis Rand. Obviously, I have more than a passing interest in the subject and would not be writing this book if I did not consider Rand's works significant. However, I am not a spokesperson for Objectivism, nor am I a student of Objectivism if by that one means that one is studying the subject in the hopes of being acknowledged as one of its spokespeople. What I am is a literary critic and scholar who has published widely about Rand and other twentieth-century writers. Just as some writers choose to study the works of Ernest Hemingway or F. Scott Fitzgerald and become Hemingway or Fitzgerald scholars, so I have, in this instance, chosen to study the works of Ayn Rand, but I would no more think of becoming a follower of Rand than I would choose to follow Hemingway, much as I admire his work.

Ayn Rand can, however, be compared to Hemingway and Fitzgerald in that her public persona came to be as well known and defined as the most carefully created fictional character. Just as the flaming, hell-bent-for-leather, jazz-age johnny became indistinguishable in the public mind from the hard-drinking, fountain-swimming Scott and the "macho," adventuresome Hemingway hero was outswaggered by "Papa" himself, so Ayn Rand became the quintessential Rand heroine. She presented herself as representative of her fictional ideal: rational, objective, uncompromising, unswerving. Her followers can find no imperfections. This tends to create a situation in which all who are not fully in accord with Rand are seen as part of the opposition.

Given these difficulties, I have attempted to remain as neutral as possible. I was originally asked to consider this project by a former research editor for Greenwood Press, who, having read my 1978 article about Rand, "Ayn Rand and Feminism," published in *College English*, concluded that I could produce the appropriate research guide.[4] When I was being considered to write the Ayn Rand entry for *American Women Writers*, I was carefully screened by Lina Mainiero, the editor, and Frederick Ungar, the publisher.[5]

Objectivity does not preclude judgment, however, and on those occasions where evaluation is suitable, I have not hesitated to convey my conclusions. In those cases, I have taken pains to delineate clearly when Rand's works are being summarized and when the opinions are those of the author. Some chapters are naturally more subjective than others. In the chapter on criticism of Rand's works, for example, I consider it appropriate to point out the prejudices of particular reviewers as well as obvious faults in their approaches. On all occasions where I have paraphrased or represented Rand's views, I have attempted to be accurate in matter and tone.

If I were to choose an alternate title for this volume, I would call it *A Guide to the Works of Ayn Rand*. The word "guide" suggests steering, piloting, or conducting. It is my hope that this work will serve to conduct readers to the primary sources that are the writings of Rand, herself.

Even the most ingenious description is no substitute for the thing itself, though it may help you decide whether or not you wish to investigate the subject further.

The organization of this *Companion* follows a logical heuristic: Who? What? and So what? "Who is Ayn Rand?" is the question answered partly by the brief biographical chapter. The main body of this book, however, responds to the question "What has she written?" That is covered in the chapters on her fiction, her nonfiction, and in the compendium of characters. It is also part of the rationale for the bibliography. "So what?" is the question that calls for critical reaction and that is provided in the chapter on criticism. It is also addressed by those sections of the bibliography that list works about Rand by others. The appendix provides a listing of works by authors who were favorably reviewed in Objectivist publications. That data would be interesting for readers who wish to expand their list of authors "simpatico" to Rand.

NOTES

1. The answer to my request for an interview was a letter from her lawyers threatening to sue me for copyright infringement. This was obviously a ploy to discourage my project, as they had not seen a word I had written. Dr. William F. O'Neill of the University of Southern California had a similar experience when he was writing *With Charity Toward None*. Rand's lawyers also threatened to take him to court. O'Neill suspects "that the threat of litigation is primarily a matter of intimidation." His book was published in 1971 and, to date, he has not been sued, nor have I. In one of those ironic confluences of the literary world, I met Eugene Winnick, the lawyer who wrote me the threatening letter, some years later in Tuscaloosa, Alabama, at a conference marking the 50th anniversary of the publication of Steinbeck's *The Grapes of Wrath*. Winnick was then head of MacIntosh and Otis, the firm that represented Steinbeck's works, which are another of my research interests. Our interchange was quite friendly.

2. "Court Upholds Use of Author's Name in Blurb," *Publisher's Weekly*, 31 March 1969, 35. Rand sued Avon Books for invasion of privacy because they used her name on the jacket blurb for *Chaos Below Heaven* by Eugene Vale. The blurb, which quoted a review in the *San Francisco Examiner*, compared Rand and Vale. The court ruled against her; the majority opinion was that when one is a public figure in the literary world "the right to discuss her work, to comment on it, to criticize and compare is thrown into the public domain."

3. "A Statement of Policy: Part 1," *The Objectivist*, June 1968.

4. Letter from Art Stickney, 26 January 1979.

5. Letter from Lina Mainiero, 12 May 1977. Mainiero, a senior editor at Frederick Ungar Publishing Company, expressed concern about "the nature of your reaction to Rand's work." Although Mainiero was opposed to Rand's theories, she had "affectionate feelings" for her as a person and did not want what she characterized as "vicious and unfair attacks" replicated in the *American Women Writers* volume. Mainero wished to be assured that I was "still fairly open-

minded about her." I sent her copies of what I had written about Rand, which convinced her of my ability to handle the subject with equanimity. (See Mimi Gladstein, "Ayn Rand," in *American Women Writers*, Vol. 3, ed. Lina Mainiero [New York: Frederick Ungar Publishing Co., 1981], 438–39.) Since the publication of the first edition of this *Companion*, I have received unsolicited letters and materials from people all over the country. In some cases those letters included information they hoped would be helpful for a future edition. In other cases, they were just expressions of appreciation for the book as an impartial resource. Further evidence of my status as independent scholar is my "Sidelights" essay for the 1989 *Contemporary Authors* reference book. It has been well received by people on all sides of the Objectivist endeavor. I was also invited by Twayne Publishing to write the forthcoming Masterworks Studies volume on *Atlas Shrugged*.

CHAPTER 1

Biographical Data

The woman who came to be known as Ayn Rand was born Alisa (Alice) Rosenbaum in St. Petersburg, Russia, on February 2, 1905.[1] The full name, according to the official dossier attesting to her completion of studies at the University of Petrograd, is Alisa Zinovievna Rosenbaum.[2] Her family was nominally Jewish, but her father, Zinovy Zacharovich (Fronz), was nonreligious and her mother, Anna Borisovna, only perfunctorily so. There is little evidence that Rand received any traditional religious upbringing. Early in life she developed an antipathy to all religions, which she branded as mysticism. By the age of fourteen, she had declared herself an atheist. The Rosenbaum family was comfortably fixed, and Rand received a good education, attending both gymnasium and the university. Rand remembers herself as an outstanding student, one whose intellectual abilities flowered early. She claims that her recollections about herself begin at the age of two and a half.[3] She could read and write before she entered elementary school.

Before the Communist Revolution, her family enjoyed the benefits of their affluence. They vacationed at country resorts or traveled abroad. It was during one of the family excursions to London that Rand made up her mind to be a writer. She had spent an evening alone in the hotel room, totally taken up with creating adventures for a group of women she had seen on a musical revue advertisement. When she realized that by creating stories for these characters she was doing what writers do, she decided that writing would be her profession. Though she was an outstanding math student and majored in history at the university, she never wavered from her goal. Almost a half century later, Rand explained that plot was the essential structuring element in her writing. She wrote, "I write—and read—for the sake of the story."[4]

Her father owned a small pharmacy in St. Petersburg, which was nationalized by the Communist government when Ayn was twelve years old. Life changed drastically for them after that. What had been St. Petersburg became Petrograd and eventually Leningrad. But more changed than a name. Goods became scarce; there were long lines for basic necessities. More terrible than the material deprivations were the spiritual constrictions of the basic Communist philosophy that people should live for the state. For a person of Rand's beliefs, that was a morally repugnant premise.

By her own accounts, Rand was a single-minded individualist from early childhood. She was not interested in the same "mindless" activities that delighted her schoolmates. She formed her ideals of human potential early; her first hero was the protagonist of a children's serial adventure story.[5] His name was Cyrus, and the character Kira, in her first novel *We the Living*, bears the feminine equivalent of his name. Cyrus inspired Rand because he was symbolic of man as he could be if he lived for the best that was in him, if he lived to his full potential. When she began to write, she created heroes modeled after Cyrus. As she explained in "The Goal of My Writing," and reiterated on numerous occasions, "The motive and purpose of my writing is *the projection of an ideal man.*"[6]

Her maturity as a child and the childlike wonder she was able to maintain as an adult are but two of the singular qualities of the unusual woman that was Ayn Rand. Writer and publisher Bennett Cerf, who readily admits that he could never win an argument with her, recounts the time he bought her a $1.00 bracelet which made her "happy as a child." He compared her to a twelve-year-old girl in the pleasure she could derive from simple things.[7]

Life in Communist Russia was unbearable for the young woman, whose notebooks were already full of outlines for the novels she was later to write. But it was not only the Communist government that filled Rand with hostility toward the country of her birth. There were other features of life in Russia that were anathema to her. During a television interview, she characterized Russia as "the ugliest, and incidentally, the most mystical country on earth." When she left it, the primary feeling she had for it was "complete loathing."[8]

Rand left Soviet Russia in 1926. She had graduated from the University of Petrograd two years earlier and then attended the State Institute of Cinema Arts, where she studied acting and screenwriting. Her twenty-first birthday was spent in transit to the United States. The occasion for her leaving was an invitation from her Portnoy family relatives to visit them in Chicago. Her mother, sensitive to her daughter's need for a context that would not inhibit her freedom, had arranged for the invitation, selling her jewelry to pay for the first-class ticket.[9]

Rand had always dreamed of America; she considered New York City the greatest city in the world. Its skyline was indicative to her of the wonders that the human mind was capable of creating. Alisa Rosenbaum accepted the invitation for what was euphemistically called a visit, but there was never any doubt in her mind that she would not return to live in Russia. The principles upon which the United States was founded—an individual's right to life, liberty, and the pursuit of happiness—were, in Rand's mind the only proper basis for government. When she arrived in this country she did not know how she would manage it, but she had decided to stay in America. She arrived in the country as Alisa Rosenbaum, but before long, all that remained of her former self were the initials A. R. There is reason to believe that the name Rand is an abbreviation of her Russian surname, though the story that she had taken the name from her Remington-Rand typewriter has general currency.[10] Her first name, Ayn, which is pronounced to rhyme with *pine*, has been explained as coming from a Finnish author, although more than one writer has suggested that being unique as she was, the Ayn is a curious spelling of "ein," German for *one*. There is coincidental biographical support for the latter. She did spend her twenty-first birthday in Berlin, a day she characterized as the first of her new life.

Rand did not remain in Chicago for long. Her goal was to become a writer, and as she was not yet accomplished in her new tongue, she decided to try to write for the silent screen. American movies such as *The Mark of Zorro* and *The Island of Lost Ships* were among her favorite diversions in Russia.[11] She moved to Los Angeles, and in a scene straight out of a Hollywood movie, she met Cecil B. De Mille on her second day in town, after her only lead for work in Hollywood had fizzled. He offered her a job as an extra on the set of his movie *The King of Kings*. There, in a romantic turn of events, she met a bit player, the man who was to be her husband and devoted companion until his death, almost three years before her own.

Though there is not much public evidence to corroborate Rand's vaunted opinion of Frank O'Connor, she always characterized him as her "top value." He was a handsome man, a kind man, decent, and gentle, but by all evidence unassertive, passive, and not at all like the Rand version of an ideal man. In later years, he became dependent on alcohol. Nathaniel Branden, who feels that between 1950 and 1968 he knew Frank O'Connor better than anyone other than Ayn Rand did, describes him as "a very, very passive man . . . not intellectually inclined . . . not motivated by powerful purposes in any sense."[12] Branden expressed great affection for O'Connor as well as the belief that he had much unrealized artistic talent. Rand steadfastly maintained, however, that her "every hero was modeled after him."[13] When Charles Francis O'Connor died in 1979 at the age of eighty-two, he was known as the "husband of the writer Ayn Rand." His obituary noted that he had appeared in several motion pictures and been a member of the Art Students

League from 1955 to 1966. Rand's unrealistic depiction of her husband is one of the areas in which she appears to have contradicted her principle of never faking reality.

Whatever the realities of Frank O'Connor's public persona, in him Ayn Rand found a spiritual soul mate, a man who would be with her in a way no one else was with her, a man who remained devoted and supportive through a fifty-year marriage. Though O'Connor was not articulate about his philosophy in the way that Rand was, he was in agreement with her about basic principles. They were married in 1929, and as the wife of an American citizen, Rand's application for citizenship was greatly facilitated. The Library of Congress lists Alice O'Connor as Rand's legal name.

Success did not come to Ayn Rand early. She worked as an extra and a junior screenwriter, on and off, until De Mille closed his independent studio in 1928. She then did odd jobs such as wait tables and stuff envelopes until she got a position in the wardrobe department of RKO Pictures. Bennett Cerf tells the story of Ayn Rand, some twenty years later, reminding his wife Phyllis Fraser that she had been the one to hand Fraser her costumes when Fraser was a starlet at RKO.[14] Rand stayed with RKO until 1932, when her first full-length, original screenplay, "Red Pawn," was sold to Universal Pictures. The screenplay was never made into a movie. She then began doing screenwriting jobs for Universal Pictures, Paramount Pictures, and Metro-Goldwyn-Mayer.[15] On her own time, she was working on several projects. Her first play, originally titled *Penthouse Legend*, was renamed *Night of January 16th* when it was produced on Broadway. It was completed in 1933, as was *We the Living*, her first novel.

These first successes established a pattern that was to reoccur through much of Rand's professional career. Regardless of what pressures were brought to bear, regardless of how many of those in power told her that she must change her style, regardless of what obstacles she found to "doing it her way," Rand remained true to her purposes in writing. Her screenplays were returned to her as improbable; one publishing house after another rejected her novel. Still, when a Broadway producer wanted to buy her play with the standard proviso that he could make changes as necessary, she rejected his offer in favor of a less lucrative offer for a Hollywood production that would not change the character of the play. It was only after the Hollywood production, when A. H. Woods renewed his offer to produce the play on Broadway, that Rand signed a contract by which she hoped she could retain artistic control. Against her better judgment, and because her agent assured her that changes could only be made by mutual consent, Rand signed with Woods and therein began a relationship that Rand was later to refer to as "hell."[16] She and Woods were at constant odds about changes and deletions he wanted to make.

Rand called the resultant product "an incongruous mongrel slapdashed out of contradictory elements."[17] Although the play had a successful run on Broadway, Rand took no pleasure in what she called its mangled corpse. It was not until 1968, when she published what was close to her original version, that she was satisfied to put her name on the title page. In 1936, Rand sued Woods for withholding some of her royalty monies to pay another writer for rewrites. She won her case.[18]

Rand and her husband moved to New York in 1934 to await the production of *Night of January 16th*. While she was living in New York, she completed the manuscript of *Anthem*. It was rejected by American publishers; the original printing was by Cassell in England in 1938. Only after Rand had made her name with *The Fountainhead*, was an American edition published. In 1946, Pamphleteers, Inc., issued a revised version. Caxton Press published a hardback version in 1953.

In her early philosophic journals, Rand explores the ideas she was to expand in *The Fountainhead*. A May 15, 1934 entry contains questions about the nature of freedom and its relationship to her concept of "supreme egoism." She wrote, "What is accomplished if the man attains power and prominence at the cost of this playing down to the masses? It is not *he* that triumphs, it is not his ideas and standards."[19] She went on to explain that she did not consider individuals who were generally regarded as ambitious truly "selfish." The problem, as she saw it, was that most ambitious men of the times achieved success by pandering to the masses and in doing so negate the self, thus becoming, in her words, "selfless." The character of Gail Wynand is the personification of the man who becomes a slave to those he thinks he controls.

In 1934 she wrote in her journal, "I have to study: philosophy, higher mathematics, physics, psychology." Once she had decided that Howard Roark, her main character in *The Fountainhead* would be an architect, she immersed herself in the study of that subject. She read voraciously throughout 1936 and 1937 and, by late in 1937, was ready to gain some practical experience. In order to facilitate her exploration of the world of contemporary architecture, she worked, without pay, as a typist in the office of Eli Jacques Kahn, a famous New York architect.

While work on *The Fountainhead* was underway, Rand also completed a stage adaptation of *We the Living* that was called *The Unconquered*. Its Broadway production was not a success. She wrote another play, "Think Twice," which was not published in her lifetime and has not had a major production.

Rand acted on her commitment to capitalism, in 1940, by working full time for the election of Wendell Willkie. Willkie had characterized himself as a defender of the free enterprise system, and in Rand's mind, it was important to counter the growing collectivism that Franklin D. Roosevelt represented. It was during this campaign that Rand came to the

conclusion that those who called themselves conservatives and supporters of capitalism were often the poorest advocates for what they believed
in. In her mind, Willkie's values were betrayed by him and his staff
during the course of the election battle.

After the election Rand returned to work as a reader for Paramount
Pictures. It was a very difficult period in her life. The funds from *Night
of January 16th* had been depleted. *The Fountainhead* had been rejected by
publisher after publisher. Then Richard Mealand, a Paramount story editor, recommended the book to Archibald G. Ogden, an editor with the
Bobbs-Merrill Company.[20]

The story of the publication of *The Fountainhead* is a dramatic one.
Ogden staked his job on it after two readers gave diametrically opposed
evaluations of why it would not sell. Ogden's firm stand for publication
convinced D. L. Chambers, the head of Bobbs-Merrill, to approve signing
a contract with Rand. The contract was signed in December 1941 with a
January 1943 completion deadline.

The Fountainhead was published in May 1943. It was positively reviewed in both the *Saturday Review of Literature* and *The New York Times
Book Review*. N. L. Rothman in the *Saturday Review* compared it to *Arrowsmith* and called Rand's novel a work of "remarkable vigor and interest."[21] Lorine Pruette made analogies between *The Fountainhead* and
The Magic Mountain or *The Master Builder*. She commended Rand as a
"writer of great power," commenting, "Good novels of ideas are rare at
any time. This is the only novel of ideas written by an American woman
that I can recall."[22]

Rand credited her husband, Frank O'Connor, with providing her the
necessary emotional sustenance to complete the book. In her introduction
to the 25th anniversary edition of *The Fountainhead*, she calls him "the
fuel" for her spirit. The book is dedicated to him, and a reproduction of
his painting "Man Also Rises" adorns the cover. Rand also incorporated
some of O'Connor's real life expressions into dialog for her hero and
heroine.

Although *The Fountainhead* has become a marvel of the publishing
world, it was not an instant best-seller. Like *One Flew Over the Cuckoo's
Nest*, another underground classic, it grew by word-of-mouth, developing a popularity that asserted itself slowly on the best-seller lists. To
sustain themselves during the period shortly before and after *The Fountainhead*'s publication, Rand took a job as a script reader for Paramount
Pictures and her husband worked as a clerk in a cigar store.

The movie sale of the novel marked the change in Rand's financial
status. She asked for and got $50,000, which was a substantial price for
movie rights in the 1940s. With that financial base, she and her husband
were able to afford some luxuries after years of penurious living. Barbara
Branden's biographical essay recounts that the first thing Rand pur-

chased after she learned that Warner Brothers had bought the film rights was a mink coat. Thirty-six years later, *Look* photographed her in a mink coat in Grand Central Station, where she had researched railroad operations for *Atlas Shrugged*, her next novel.[23]

Part of Rand's contract with Warner Brothers called for her to write the screen adaptation of her novel, and she and her husband decided to return to Hollywood to do so. She finished the script in six months, but it was obviously a difficult process for her. She later said, "It was very painful psychologically and I thought, I will never do it again."[24] In 1979 when it was announced that *Atlas Shrugged* would be adapted for a television miniseries, Sterling Siliphant joined Rand as a co-author. The adaptation was never produced.

When Rand had completed the screenplay of *The Fountainhead*, she signed a contract with Hal Wallis Productions that allowed her six months a year free for her own writing, while committing her to the other six months as a contract screenwriter. She remained with Wallis Productions from 1944 through 1949, when the screen version of *The Fountainhead* was released. After 1949, Rand was able to devote herself full time to writing and lecturing.[25]

By Rand's account, her experience with the filming of *The Fountainhead* was in many ways a repetition of her trials during the production of *Night of January 16th*. When a novelist sells movie rights, she loses control of her work. Even though Rand had been hired to write the screenplay, the studio could and did demand certain changes.[26] Rand argued with all concerned to try to maintain the integrity of her vision, and she was satisfied with the result. The movie script preserves her original theme and meaning. Reviewers, on the other hand, were not impressed with the final product. Neither Gary Cooper, as Howard Roark, nor Patricia Neal, as Dominique Francon, received kind reviews. Some of the same kinds of negative criticisms that were leveled at the book were directed at the movie script: heavy-handed, haranguing, hectoring.

Although the writer/studio relationship may have been fraught with tensions, accounts of the publisher/studio relationship indicate that both cooperated to a degree hitherto unknown. Rather than issue a popularly priced edition to take advantage of the film's release, Bobbs-Merrill advised book sellers to advertise copies at the standard price. Advertisements for the movie referred to the book, and stickers were printed to place on the book jackets, reminding readers of the movie version.[27] While this may be standard practice today, it was unusual for its time.

Upon their return to California, Rand and O'Connor purchased a small ranch in Tarzana. A house that had been designed by the talented architect Richard Neutra was part of the property. *House and Garden* featured the house, which looks as if Howard Roark might have designed it, in a 1949 pictorial.[28] While Rand closeted herself writing in a study that opened onto a beautiful patio, Frank O'Connor worked long hours developing the land. He grew flowers for commercial sale and raised peacocks. By all accounts and pictures, it was a place of great natural beauty. Unfortunately, Rand was very unhappy in such a setting; since she could not drive, she felt like a prisoner in the San Fernando Valley, away from the city.[29] Although O'Connor was very happy on the ranch, Rand preferred New York City; so in 1951, they moved back there, where they remained for the rest of their lives. Frank Lloyd Wright drew preliminary sketches for a home for them to build in the New York countryside, but they never built it, preferring to live in the heart of the city.

While awaiting the production of the movie version of *The Fountainhead*, Rand had begun work on her next novel, a work that was to be the fullest explication of her philosophy, a philosophy which at that point was still unnamed. The project was so ambitious and so all-engrossing that she felt she could no longer divide her time and energies between it and her job for Hal Wallis. She secured her release from that contract and the greater part of the next decade was spent writing *Atlas Shrugged*.

Rand gave up being a screen writer in 1949 to become a full-time writer and lecturer as noted in *200 Contemporary Authors*. However, its record of her significant public lectures does not begin until 1960, when she appeared at Yale, Princeton, and Columbia. During the 1950s, until the publication of *Atlas Shrugged* in 1957, media attention to Rand was scant. A marked increase in media coverage began in the late 1950s and reached its apex in the 1960s. Rand had become not only a best-selling author, but also the leader of an intellectual movement. The story of the transition from private person to public persona is the story of one of the most significant relationships in Rand's life.

In 1950, a nineteen-year-old psychology student at UCLA named Nathan Blumenthal wrote Rand a fan letter. Rand, who often answered letters from fans, was so impressed by the perspicacity of the young man's questions that she suggested he make an appointment to speak with her in person. Blumenthal (who subsequently adopted the name Nathaniel Branden) called Rand and so began an interaction that had a profound effect on both their lives. The first printing of *Atlas Shrugged* is dedicated to both Frank O'Connor and Nathaniel Branden; in an afterword, Rand describes Branden as her "ideal reader" and "intellectual heir." While her husband could comprehend and empathize with all of her ideas, Branden could articulate them and expand upon them.

This relationship is material for much speculation that is intellectually seductive if academically irrelevant. Would Rand have published any more fiction if she had not met Branden? Would she have become the *enfant terrible* of American philosophy? Of course, such questions are unanswerable. We do know that *Atlas Shrugged* was her last work of fiction to see print in her lifetime. After 1957 Rand published only essays and works of philosophy. We do know that after its publication Nathaniel Branden began teaching Rand's philosophy and, until their break in 1968, was the chief purveyor of her ideas. In the 1960s Rand became the matrix of a philosophical and cultural movement that grew so strong that it was characterized by detractors as both cult and religion. The nucleus of that group was provided by Nathaniel and Barbara Branden.

Barbara Branden (born Weidman), philosophy student *cum* writer, was also attending UCLA in 1950. Mutual interest in *The Fountainhead* was what originally brought Nathaniel and Barbara together when they had met two years earlier in Winnepeg, Canada. After his initial meeting with Rand, Nathaniel requested and was granted permission to bring along his friend Barbara, who was also a *Fountainhead* fan, to meet Rand. Thus began a relationship of great significance in Rand's subsequent career, one by which she was introduced to other individuals whose lives became inextricably bound up with hers.

Many of Rand's earliest close disciples, the group she called "the children" or "the class of '43," were friends and relatives of the Brandens.[30] Leonard Peikoff, then a philosophy student, is Barbara Branden's first cousin, and it was Barbara who first introduced him to Rand. Elayne Kalberman, who became the first circulation manager for *The Objectivist Newsletter*, is Nathaniel Branden's sister. Her husband Harry Kalberman, a broker, was part of the group. Joan Mitchell and Barbara Branden had been girlhood friends. Mitchell, an artist, was first married to Alan Greenspan, an economic consultant then, later chair of the Federal Reserve. Her second husband is Allan Blumenthal, a psychiatrist and cousin of Nathaniel Branden.

From its onset, the friendship among Ayn Rand, Frank O'Connor, Barbara Branden, and Nathaniel Branden was a strong one. Barbara and Nathaniel visited the California ranch regularly and were accorded the singular honor of reading the first chapters of *Atlas Shrugged* as it was being written. After a year and a half of very close association in California, Barbara and Nathaniel moved to New York to continue their studies at New York University. Not long afterwards, Ayn Rand and Frank O'Connor also moved to New York. In 1953 when Barbara and Nathaniel were married, Ayn Rand and Frank O'Connor were their matron of honor and best man.

In New York, with the Brandens as catalysts, a group began forming around Rand. Besides the individuals already mentioned, there were other professionals such as the writer/journalist Edith Efron and Mary Ann Rukavina, an art historian. Robert and Beatrice Hessen, who became the owners of the Palo Alto Book Service, joined the group later. They met with Rand to discuss her philosophy and its application to their various professions. Slowly, Rand began letting all the members of the group read *Atlas Shrugged* in its manuscript form. In those meetings, the nascent Objectivist movement was nurtured.

The publication of *Atlas Shrugged* in October of 1957 set the stage for enlarging the circle. Publication of *The Fountainhead* had engendered a stream of fan letters from readers asking questions about the amplification of Rand's ideas. That stream became a flood after the publication of *Atlas Shrugged*, and Nathaniel Branden conceived the idea of using the letters as a starting place for the teaching of Ayn Rand's basic philosophical principles. He prepared a twenty-lecture course of study that he called Nathaniel Branden Lectures. "Basic Principles of Objectivism" was taught for the first time in the spring of 1958. What followed was a most unusual success story and the birth of a movement.

With Nathaniel Branden as president and Barbara Branden as everything else, a class of twenty-eight students grew into a burgeoning business. When Nathaniel Branden Lectures became incorporated as Nathaniel Branden Institute (NBI), a miniculture was born. Not only the Brandens but other kindred professionals taught courses that were taped and later offered in cities all over the country. NBI had a publication branch that published appropriate essays and monographs and a book service that sold approved books. In conjunction with Ayn Rand, the Brandens inaugurated *The Objectivist Newsletter*. At its zenith, NBI sponsored dances, fashion shows, and sports events. There was even an NBI Theatre, which showed vintage romantic movies.[31] By the time it disbanded, the Nathaniel Branden Institute, which originally had its office on the Branden's dining room table, occupied a suite in the Empire State Building.

The Nathaniel Branden Institute was a business with a purpose; that purpose was changing the world. Objectivism was the foundation upon which this new world was to be erected. During the 1960s, Objectivism, which Rand characterized as an intellectual movement, grew phenomenally. Its influence was far-reaching. Besides those who identified themselves as Objectivists or students of Objectivism, there were admirers of Rand, who while taking exception to the close monitoring of her ideas, could still credit her with inspiring them in positive directions. Although she rejected them, many members of the Libertarian movement acknowledge their intellectual debt to her philosophy.

The 1960s were the heyday of Rand's public career. She received a Doctor of Humane Letters at Lewis and Clark College; she lectured at prestigious universities such as Harvard, MIT, and Johns Hopkins University. She was a regular speaker at the Ford Hall Forum in Boston, a *Playboy* interviewee, and bumper stickers displayed *Atlas Shrugged*'s opening question, "Who is John Galt?" Rand conveyed her ideas on her own radio programs; she wrote a newspaper column, edited a newsletter which grew into a journal, and published a number of books on her philosophy. She attracted a large number of followers; her philosophy and following frightened those who opposed her ideas. She was adored; she was reviled.

Rand had never been a social being. The kind of human interaction she enjoyed was intellectual. On a one-to-one basis she was charismatic. She had the ability to charm even those who were strongly opposed to her ideas. Writers Clifton Fadiman and George Axelrod were taken with her.[32] Popular novelist John O'Hara wrote his daughter that Rand, whom he had heard described as a "terror," was "Fun, actually."[33] Intellectually, she could best anyone in an argument. Hiram Haydn, Rand's editor at Random House, complains in his autobiography that in his dealings with Rand he always ended up feeling like her "concept of the soft-headed, ambivalent, tortured liberal!"[34] Bennett Cerf concurred, "You can't argue with Ayn Rand. She's so clever at it, she makes a fool out of you."[35]

Another characteristic of Rand's interpersonal relationships was their impermanence. Jerome Tuccille satirizes what he calls her "purges" and re-creates fictionalized scenes in which both historian Leonard Liggio and economist Murray Rothbard are expunged from Rand's inner circle for their deviationism.[36] Barbara Branden calls these interpersonal ruptures "breaks" and recalls that Rand even broke with the sister she had brought from Russia after nearly a half century's separation.[37] The break with Edith Efron was one of the earliest excommunications. Rand also broke with Henry Mark Holzer (her lawyer) and with Bennett Cerf. Cerf, who thought Rand a brilliant and remarkable woman, blamed what he called "her sycophants" for her imperious ways. He theorized that all the adulation made her opinionated, autocratic, and convinced of her omniscience.[38] Although those characteristics may have been exacerbated by her place at the head of an intellectual movement, the supreme egoism and the strong convictions are evident long before she became famous.

The most significant break in terms of the effect on both Rand's personal and professional life was in 1968, when Rand repudiated both Nathaniel and Barbara Branden in an *Objectivist* article "To Whom It May Concern." Allan Blumenthal, Alan Greenspan, Leonard Peikoff, and Mary Ann (Rukavina) Sures joined her in the public condemnation and repudiation. The Brandens, who by that time were in the process of a divorce, responded in separate letters "In Answer to Ayn Rand." An important factor in the break was the fact that Nathaniel Branden had developed a serious relationship with Patrecia Gullison, which he kept secret from Rand.[39] Besides deception, Rand accused Branden of serious psycho-epistemological problems and of profiting from the "gold mine" of her name.[40] The Brandens' responses counter Rand's accusations. Nathaniel Branden hints that the real problem is that he rejected Rand's romantic advances.[41] Barbara Branden, while expressing regret at having to choose between Ayn Rand and the principles Rand taught her, and acknowledging the wrongness of Nathaniel's deception, describes what she saw as the contradictions in Rand's behavior and accusations.[42]

Although many may have suspected the real nature of the Rand/Branden break, the public acknowledgment of the full story did not come until Barbara Branden's 1986 biography *The Passion of Ayn Rand* and Nathaniel Branden's subsequent publication, three years later, of *Judgment Day*, his version of the events. According to both, a sexual affair between Ayn and Nathaniel began early in 1955.[43] At the onset of the affair, both Frank O'Connor and Barbara Branden were informed and convinced to acquiesce in the secrecy and scheduling of trysts. Ayn and Nathaniel conducted their rendezvous in the Rand/O'Connor apartment until Rand's post-publication depression that followed the reception of *Atlas Shrugged* reduced the regularity of their meetings. According to both Brandens, the 1968 break-up was precipitated by Ayn's desire to resume the romantic aspects of the relationship, whereas Nathaniel Branden had secretly fallen in love with Patrecia, who was to become his second wife.

When the fireworks were over, Leonard Peikoff had replaced Nathaniel Branden as Rand's heir. He became associate editor of *The Objectivist* and the main teacher of Objectivist courses. He was subsequently a contributing editor for *The Ayn Rand Letter*. Afterwards, he became consulting editor for *The Intellectual Activist* and *The Objectivist Forum*. Currently, he is chairman emeritus of The Ayn Rand Institute, founded in 1985 to serve as a center for the advancement of Objectivism. Peikoff, as Rand's literary executor, has continued to publish much previously unpublished material. *The Early Ayn Rand* (1984), is a selection of her unpublished fiction; *The Voice of Reason: Essays in Objectivist Thought* (1988) contains essays by Rand, previously published, but heretofore unanthologized. *Letters of Ayn Rand* (1995), edited by Michael S. Berliner, and *Journals of Ayn Rand* (1997), edited by David Harriman, are more additions to the posthumous oeuvre. *The Ayn Rand Reader* (1999), co-edited by Peikoff and Gary Hull, excerpts both fiction and nonfiction. *Russian Writings on Hollywood* (1999), edited by Michael S. Berliner, is a translation of works she wrote before she left her native land. Even her marginalia have been turned into a book.

The Objectivist movement was profoundly affected by the rupture that pitted friends and family against each other. Rand's general popularity, however, was largely unaffected. She continued to publish her reactions to contemporary events, her essays were gathered into books and published, and she was a much sought-after speaker. In 1974 she was the graduation speaker at West Point. In 1979 NBC announced plans to develop a television miniseries based on *Atlas Shrugged*. Rand fans eagerly awaited its network production. Subsequent years have brought stories about impending productions, but as of this writing, nothing has materialized.[44]

During the 1970s both Ayn Rand and Frank O'Connor suffered from health problems. The cigarettes that had served Rand effectively as a dramatic symbol in fiction served her ill in real life. She developed lung cancer, requiring surgery. O'Connor's condition, exacerbated by heavy drinking, worsened. Rand stopped publishing *The Ayn Rand Letter*, but she continued to write and lecture.

Frank O'Connor died in November 1979. Rand remained true to her principles. When asked on a Phil Donahue show shortly after her husband's death if she wished there were an afterlife so she could see him again, she promptly replied, "Oh no, if I believed that, I would kill myself right now so I could be with him." She remained alert and active in her later years. Her last speech was in November 1981 at the conference of the National Committee for Monetary Reform. Although her health was precarious, she was still scheduled to lecture at the Ford Hall Forum the following spring. Leonard Peikoff delivered that speech; Ayn Rand died in her apartment on March 6, 1982.

NOTES

1. I am indebted to Barbara Branden who provided me with pre-publication information about the essential facts of Rand's life for the first edition of *The Ayn Rand Companion*. Branden, who wrote Rand's only authorized biography as the title essay of *Who Is Ayn Rand?*, also published *The Passion of Ayn Rand*, a book-length independent biography in 1986. Branden calls Rand "Alice," the English equivalent of the Russian "Alisa."

2. Chris Matthew Sciabarra, *Ayn Rand: The Russian Radical* (University Park, PA: Pennsylvania State University Press, 1995), 396f. Sciabarra cites the Archive of the University of Leningrad as his source and spells the name Alissa. *Ayn Rand: A Sense of Life* (Layton, UT: Gibbs Smith, 1998), Michael Paxton's book version of the film documentary of her life, made with the cooperation of The Ayn Rand Institute, spells her name Alisa.

3. Appearance, *Tomorrow*, NBC Television, 2 July 1979.

4. Ayn Rand, "The Goal of My Writing," in *The Romantic Manifesto* (New York: The World Publishing Company, 1969), 162.

5. Maurice Champagne-Gilbert's *Vallée Mysterieuse* (*The Mysterious Valley*), with its original illustrations by Rene Giffey, translated by Bill Bucko, and with an introduction by Harry Binswanger, has been published by The Atlantean Press in Lafayette, Colorado, in 1994. The hero Cyrus is one of a group of British officers in India.

6. *Romantic Manifesto*, 161.

7. Bennet Cerf, *At Random* (New York: Random House, 1977), 252.

8. Appearance, *Donahue*, WGN-TV Chicago, IL, 29 April 1980.

9. *Ayn Rand: A Sense of Life*, 53.

10. "Impact" (May 1997), the newsletter of The Ayn Rand Institute, carries a story about recent archival materials that suggest Rand selected her professional name before she left Russia. It cites letters from family in Russia that refer to the name "Rand" before they had heard from her from America. It also cites a *New York Evening Post* story in which Rand states that fact. In the cyrillic spelling of her name are resemblances to both the names "Ayn" and "Rand."

11. Barbara Branden, *Who Is Ayn Rand?* (New York: Paperback Library, 1962), 135.

12. Personal interview with Nathaniel Branden, Beverly Hills, CA, 12 October 1981.

13. Quoted in the obituary "Charles Francis O'Connor, Artist, Husband of the Writer, Ayn Rand," *New York Times*, 12 November 1979, D11.

14. Cerf, 252.

15. *200 Contemporary Authors* (Detroit MI: Gale Research Co., 1969), 225.

16. "Introduction," *Night of January 16th* (New York: New American Library, 1968), 8.

17. Ibid.

18. "Author Wins Royalty Row," *New York Times*, 11 February 1936, 19.

19. "From Ayn Rand's Unpublished Writings: Philosophical Journal," *The Objectivist Forum*, August 1983, 5.

20. B. Branden, *Who Is Ayn Rand?*, 160.

21. N. L. Rothman, "H. Roark, Architect," review of *The Fountainhead, Saturday Review of Literature*, 29 May 1943, 31.

22. Lorine Pruette, "Battle Against Evil," review of *The Fountainhead, The New York Times Book Review*, 13 May 1943, 7.

23. "Ayn Rand Returns," *Look*, 14 May 1979, 72.

24. Ibid.

25. *200 Contemporary Authors*, 225.

26. Kevin McGann, "Ayn Rand in the Stockyard of the Spirit," in *The Modern American Novel and the Movies*, ed. Gerald Peary and Roger Shatzkin (New York: Frederick Ungar Publishing Co., 1978), 328. McGann feels that Rand's script compromises the integrity of Dominique's character and panders to middle-class mores in two significant ways: Dominique does not marry Peter and her adultery and its public acknowledgment are avoided by having Wynand commit suicide.

27. Paul S. Nathan, "Books into Films," *Publisher's Weekly*, 11 June 1949, 2405.

28. "A Steel House with a Suave Finish," *House and Garden*, August 1949, 54–57.

29. Personal interview with Barbara Branden, Los Angeles, CA, 9 November 1981.

30. Lewis Nichols, "Class of '43," *New York Times*, 22 December 1957, sec. 7, 8.

31. B. Branden, interview.

32. Cerf, 250.

33. Finis Farr, *O'Hara: A Biography* (Boston: Little, Brown and Company, 1973), 262.

34. Hiram Haydn, *Words and Faces* (New York: Harcourt Brace Jovanovich, 1974), 261.

35. Cerf, 251.

36. Jerome Tuccille, *It Usually Begins with Ayn Rand* (New York: Stein and Day, 1972), 27–33.

37. B. Branden, interview.

38. Cerf, 251.

39. Patrecia Gullison became Patricia Scott, when she married Larry Scott shortly after Nathaniel Branden met her. She then adopted the professional name of Patrecia Wynand, at Rand's suggestion, after Gail Wynand in *The Fountainhead* (Nathaniel Branden, *Judgment Day* [Boston: Houghton Mifflin, 1989], 364).

40. Ayn Rand, "To Whom It May Concern," *The Objectivist*, 7, no. 5 (May 1968): 1–8.

41. Nathaniel Branden, "In Answer to Ayn Rand," mailing to subscribers to *The Objectivist*, October 1968.

42. Barbara Branden, "In Answer to Ayn Rand," mailing to the subscribers to *The Objectivist*, October 1968.

43. Barbara Branden, *Passion of Ayn Rand* (Garden City, NY: Doubleday, 1986), 272; N. Branden, *Judgment Day*, 158.

44. John Aglialoro leased the rights to *Atlas Shrugged* from Leonard Peikoff. He told an audience at the "Atlas and the World" Conference in October 1997 that his lease runs out in ten years.

Wedding of Nathaniel and Barbara Branden, New York City, January 10, 1953. Frank O'Connor, best man, has his back to the camera. Ayn Rand is matron of honor.

Barbara Branden and Ayn Rand in Barbara Branden's apartment, New York City, in the mid-1960s.

CHAPTER 2

The Fiction

Although Ayn Rand became known as a philosopher whose ideas influenced people as diverse as politicians and tennis superstars, she was initially a writer of fiction. It was through her fiction that her ideas were first disseminated, and it is still through her works of fiction that the majority of readers are introduced to her essential concepts. Although there are those readers who recognize such titles as *The Romantic Manifesto* or *The Virtue of Selfishness*, rare are the individuals who, if they have not read at least one of Rand's novels, have not heard of *Anthem*, *The Fountainhead*, or *Atlas Shrugged*. The latter titles are still in print in hardcover as well as in paperback. Rand's nonfiction works, while still immensely popular, do not compare in sales to her fiction.

Rand's fiction is her foremost achievement. It has made her a world-class author. It is the medium through which her message is most widely and most palatably broadcast. Even those who oppose her politically and philosophically acknowledge the impact of her fiction.

Although Rand has not published much in comparison to other writers of similar popularity, what she has written continues to sell remarkably well. Her popularity transcends the generations. The sales figures continue to be a publishing phenomenon.

During her lifetime, Rand published four novels, one play, and one short story. After her death, samplings of her early writings, some of it done before she had mastered the language, were published in an anthology of unpublished fiction, *The Early Ayn Rand*, a compilation of some short stories, plays, and a synopsis for a movie. Also included is material excised from the published versions of two of her novels. *Journals of Ayn Rand* includes unpublished scenarios and a synopsis for a proposed screenplay, "Top Secret."

Rand's major literary works follow similar plot patterns. In each, an exceptionally able and individualistic protagonist battles the forces of collectivism and mediocrity that are threatening or have destroyed a nation or the world. Although Rand personally became more pessimistic about the prospects for individualism in the real world (in 1975 she ceased publishing her newsletter with the announcement that the state of culture was so low and that so many of the dire events that she had predicted had occurred, that to continue to write about and warn of them would be redundant), in her fictional worlds, the plot structures become, chronologically, more optimistic. Of course, she quit writing fiction in 1957, nearly a generation before she stopped publishing her newsletter.

Her initial works hold out little hope. In her first published work, *Night of January 16th*, the outcome for the protagonist is dubious. There is a new jury for each performance and Karen Andre's fate hangs on the "sense of life" of a different dozen jurors nightly. Whether or not she is convicted, her main value in life, Bjorn Faulkner, is dead. *We the Living*, begun earlier, but published later, has a very depressing ending. Of the three major characters, two die and the third is on his way to sure self-destruction. It is not until *Anthem* that the worthwhile people begin winning. At the end of that novelette, although the world is still in a benighted state, the young Edenic couple has escaped and are ready to establish a refuge for others of their ilk, thereby holding forth hope for the future. *The Fountainhead* paints a roseate picture. Not only does Howard Roark prosper, but Dominique Francon, who had been convinced that the world would destroy anyone with his integrity, has changed her mind and become his wife. The most optimistic ending is reserved for *Atlas Shrugged*. Although Roark succeeds in *The Fountainhead*, the Ellsworth Tooheys of the world are still solidly in place. In *Atlas Shrugged*, however, the strike of the "men of the mind" vanquishes the looters, leeches, and "second-handers," leaving the world firmly in the hands of the creative and the productive.

A character-by-character analysis is provided in chapter three. Some general commentary should suffice here. Of Rand's five protagonists, three are women and two are men. However, the great preponderance of her other characters, major and minor, are male. Her main female characters share certain characteristics: They have slender physiques, defiant stances, and inner calm. The major male characters have distinctive coloring and bearing: John Galt's hair is chestnut-brown, and his eyes are deep gray in a face that reflects no pain, fear, or guilt; Francisco d'Anconia has black hair, blue eyes, and lots of style; Howard Roark's hair is a startling orange, and his eyes are gray; Andrei Taganov's face carries a battle scar and projects the look of a caged tiger. Gray eyes predominate as do supple and hard physiques. Rand's heroes are tall, straight, and strong. As with their feminine counterparts, defiance is a keystone to their characters. Fear is never part of their demeanor. In fact, they are often depicted with whip imagery: Bjorn Faulkner treats Karen Andre as if she were an animal he was trying to break; Leo Kovalensky is described as being born to carry a whip. There has been a suggestion that the recurring whip imagery in Rand's fiction had its genesis in her early fascination with Hollywood movies, *The Mark of Zorro*, in particular.

Rand also uses a technique, traditional in comedy and allegory, by which characters' names are indicators of their personalities. Such names as Wesley Mouch, Ellsworth Monkton Toohey, Homer Slottern, and Balph Eubank carry strong suggestions of their wearers' offensive natures. There are, however, many villains with neutral names, such as Robert Stadler or James Taggart. Nevertheless, even if the character has a handsome physical appearance and a neutral name, the reader is never left in doubt about Rand's attitude toward him or her. Ambiguous characters are extremely rare in Rand's writing. The narrator, who is most definitely subjective, communicates quite clearly whether a character is to be viewed positively or negatively. Rand's usual method of character introduction is a brief biographical sketch in which the individual's virtues or vices are clearly delineated. Though Pavel Syerov is described as nice looking, if a bit of a dandy, the reader is quickly informed that while he represents himself as a revolutionary hero, in fact, "Pavlusha" stayed home with a cold during the initial forays of the Revolution. Lillian Rearden, whose classic beauty fools Hank Rearden into thinking she is someone to strive for, turns empty eyes and a superficial gaiety on those who encounter her. Although she claims to love her husband, she does not value what he does or appreciate his abilities.

Instant recognition of the like-minded is an ability shared by Rand's heroes and villains. Although Kira Argounova has never seen Leo Kovalensky before, she is willing to let him believe she is a prostitute rather than let him go out of her life. Equality 7–2521 and Liberty 5–3000 need only eye contact to establish a bond strong enough to make them defy their collectivist society. After minimal conversation, she is sure enough of him to follow him into the Uncharted Forest. In two of Rand's stories, the first significant meeting of hero and heroine is accompanied by a rapelike encounter, which, rather than distancing the couple, cements the relationship. Howard Roark's rape of Dominique Francon establishes an unspoken bond as neither speaks during the entire episode. Bjorn Faulkner rapes Karen Andre when she comes for a job interview, and she remains his business partner and mistress for the rest of his life. John Galt's first sexual experience with Dagny Taggart is a simulated rape in the tunnels of Taggart Transcontinental. For Rand, these romanticized rapes are symbolic of the head-on clash of two strong personalities. The rapist is conquered just as his victim is. A readership with a raised consciousness about the nature of rape might find this symbolism unpalatable.

When Rand's characters love, they love without reservation. For Rand the emotion of love is a response to values, and the object of one's love is a representation of all that one holds dear; therefore, just as a Rand character does battle for that which he or she values, so a Rand character will do anything for the loved one. This is demonstrated in each of Rand's works of fiction. In *Night of January 16th*, Karen Andre is willing to do anything for Bjorn Faulkner. She defies the law, engages in criminal acts, and even allows Bjorn to marry Nancy Whitfield, since that is what Bjorn thinks is necessary to buttress his failing financial empire. She allows herself to be tried for his murder because she thinks that she is helping him engineer a fake suicide. "Guts" Regan is also willing to help Andre and Faulkner stage the fake suicide. His reason is that he loves Karen; he loves her so much that he would help her run off with the man she loves after she has turned down his advances. As he explains to the district attorney, even a lowlife gangster such as he can be moved to nobility when "something passes us to which one kneels."

Leo's health is so important to Kira that she becomes Andrei's mistress so that she will have the money to send him to a sanatorium in the Crimea. Prior to that, she has risked her life attempting to escape with Leo, although she does not even know his name. Kira, who never lies, lies to both Andrei and Leo in order to save Leo's life and pride. She pretends that she loves Andrei, and she lies to Leo about where she gets money.

Roark, who is fiercely independent, openly acknowledges to Dominique how much she controls him. When she attempts to play power games with him, he shows her immediately that she owns him—"all . . . that can be owned." His love for her is so great that he will not ask her to be his wife because he knows that she cannot be whole until she comes to him with a healthy ego. He stands by when she marries first Peter Keating and then Gail Wynand, enduring the pain while she goes through her perverse penance.

Wynand explains to Dominique that "love is exception-making." Although he has broken every person of supposed integrity that he can find in order to prove his power, he does not want to break her. In his eyes, she is a person of integrity, who loves integrity, a "person who matches inside and out."

John Galt puts his life in danger in order to be with Dagny Taggart. Eventually his association with her results in his capture and torture. Before the government agents arrive to arrest him, he tells her that he does not regret her action in leading them to him. Dagny exclaims, "I didn't care whether either one of us lived afterwards, just to see you this once!" The life-worshipping Galt tells Dagny that he will kill himself rather than suffer the pain of seeing her tortured.

Rand's vision of the world was set when she was quite young, and she varied little from it as she grew older. She had a clear sense of the kind of individual she admired and the kind of person she wanted to be. Once she had set her goals, she worked toward them with unswerving determination and integrity. She did not compromise her values. She was determined to do it her way. As she strove to understand why people were beset by the problems they were beset by, she developed a set of principles by which she judged individuals and events. Although there are reasons to believe that she was not unswervingly consistent in her application of her own principles, she claimed that she was. The first sentence of the Afterword to *Atlas Shrugged* reads, "My personal life . . . is a postscript to my novels; it consists of the sentence: 'And I mean it!' " A detailed working out of all of Rand's major themes would occupy several books; after she stopped writing fiction, Rand published seven works of nonfiction in which she did just that. This chapter will focus only on the literary works and on some of the implications of Rand's predominant messages that can be inferred from the actions and words of Rand's fictional spokespersons.

The major theme of Rand's fiction is the primacy of the individual. The unique and precious individual human life is the standard by which good is judged. That which sustains and enriches life is good; that which negates and impoverishes the individual's pursuit of happiness is evil. All of the secondary themes in Rand's fiction develop as the logical consequence of her major theme. If the individual human life is the standard by which good is judged, then it follows that the political, economic, and religious systems and institutions that encourage and protect individual freedom and happiness are the proper systems to develop and sustain. While her major theme is explicitly developed in all of her novels, it is not until *Atlas Shrugged* that she works out all of the political, economic, and metaphysical implications of that theme. Rand repeatedly articulated her respect for America's Founding Fathers and the premises upon which the United States is based. If there is a phrase in the Declaration of Independence that synthesizes Rand's philosophy, it is the statement that each individual is endowed with certain inalienable rights: the rights to life, liberty, and the pursuit of happiness. As Rand worked out her interpretation of what those rights entailed, she saw three areas of conflict in which those rights were held in the balance.

THE THREE ANTIPODES

Individualism versus Collectivism

Egoism versus Altruism

Reason versus Mysticism

In Rand's philosophy all of these areas are interconnected. Reason is the tool by which the individual discerns that which is life sustaining and ego nourishing. Collectivism, altruism, and mysticism all work against individual freedom, a healthy ego, and rationality.

In all of Rand's works, the individual human is the most important being in the universe. Not God, nor country, nor cause precedes the individual in Rand's hierarchy of values. In her first novel, *We the Living*, she pointedly illustrates how putting one's state or political cause above the self is detrimental to human happiness and ultimately creates a poorly functioning state. That one values individuals above ideology is clearly seen in Kira's affection for Andrei. Although Kira hates Communists, she sees Andrei's worth as an individual and worries about him, expressing fear for his safety when he fights rebellious farmers.

John Whitfield, the villainous banker who kills Bjorn Faulkner, states his credo on the witness stand, "I believe in one's duty above all; Bjorn Faulkner believed in nothing but his own pleasure." One of Rand's favorite techniques is this kind of dramatic irony whereby the speaker, in trying to explain what is wrong with a character by his standards, is explaining what is right with that character by Rand's standards.

The Fountainhead is Rand's fullest explication of the primacy of the individual. One of her stated purposes in writing this novel was to develop a defense of egoism, which Rand has also called selfishness and rational self-interest. Howard Roark explains the virtue of selfishness in his defense at the Cortlandt trial. In his explanation of how independent creators have benefited humankind, he says, "The creators were not selfless. It is the whole secret to their power—that it was self-sufficient, self-motivated, self-generated." He goes on to explain that only by living for oneself can one accomplish those things that are the crown of human achievement. The mind, in which great creations are conceived, is an individual thing. "There is no such thing as a collective brain."

The much-quoted rule of living of Mulligan's Valley—the utopia of *Atlas Shrugged*—is another of the specific articulations of Rand's belief in the primacy of the individual. It is carved in granite on the door to the structure that holds the motor that could power the world, the product of one mind. The oath reads: "I swear by my life and my love of it that I will never live for the sake of another man, nor ask another man to live for mine."

Parallel to Rand's development of the dichotomy of the individual versus the collective is her working out of the analogous situation of the productive versus the parasitical. In Rand's fictional world, the elite are the able, the doers. The ability to create, to produce, to do is a primary virtue. For Rand, you are what you do. This is not as evident in her early works as it was to become in the novels that were the hallmarks of her philosophy. Bjorn Faulkner has a great financial empire, but it is not clear that this is as much a result of his productive capabilities as it is of his financial manipulations and wheeler dealing. His callous appropriation of his stockholders' funds for his own purposes is more appropriate to those that Rand was later to describe as looters than the kind of scrupulous achiever she depicts in Howard Roark. Karen Andre is an excellent secretary; she can take any shorthand assignment Bjorn Faulkner throws at her. She also becomes an expert at forging his signature. Her productive capabilities, however, are not on a par with later Rand heroines.

In *We the Living*, the only person of actual achievement is Andrei. He is a hero whose bravery has been demonstrated in battle. At the Battle of Melitopol, he risks his life to convince the White Army soldiers in the trenches that the red flag should be their flag. His recognition of like quality in another is demonstrated when he first helps and then allows Captain Karsavin, one of the ablest of the White Army leaders, to commit suicide rather than risk capture. Though Kira and Leo have the raw materials for later achievement, neither of them is allowed to develop those natural resources. Kira has grand aspirations; she wants to be an engineer and build bridges and buildings. To that end, she is a good student at the Technological Institute. Although the reader is convinced that she could be an able engineer, Kira is prevented from becoming one. She is expelled from the institute because she is the daughter of a former factory owner. Her talents are buried in a deadening job as an excursion guide. Leo's only demonstrated talents are in the attraction of women. Although Kira believes in him and although he does begin study at the university, his promise is also stultified by the discrimination practiced against children of those who were once in power. Leo's only accomplishments are a bitter bravado and black marketeering.

In *We the Living*, Rand had not yet fully developed her concept of the parasitical. The negative characters are more specifically opportunistic than parasitical. Of course, the opportunists are not productive; therefore, as they do not contribute materially, they are in a very real sense feeding off of the contributions of others. Not only are the Communists not productive, but their system does not promote productivity. What counts is not ability, but party membership or congeniality. Pavel Syerov trades upon his "supposed" friendship with Andrei Taganov, who is a real hero. He also benefits from the dangerous activities of speculators. They take the chances, and he is paid off. Victor Dunaev has some real abilities, but he uses them to further his political aims, not to accomplish anything concrete.

It is not until *Anthem* that the Rand hero whose abilities are society-shaking in a positive sense is introduced. Equality 7–2521 is a creator and inventor in the tradition of Galileo, Edison, and Einstein. In a world where all technological advancement has been lost, he rediscovers electricity. Through hands-on experimentation, he is able to move beyond the shackles of his limited education. Not only does he invent, but he defies. When his society is not ready to accept what he offers, he escapes through uncharted forests to form a new colony of his own where he and others who wish to throw off the chains of collectivism can develop individually.

In *Anthem*, there is really only one person of exceptional ability. There is a suggestion that International 4–8818 may be an artist with a real comic talent, and Liberty 5–3000 is brave and loyal, but the only one whose productive capabilities are fully displayed is Equality 7–2521. The villains in the story are not so much parasitical as inert and antiprogressive. They neither want to benefit from Equality 7–2521's invention, nor do they want anyone else to.

The theme of the productive versus the parasitical is developed more fully in *The Fountainhead*. The term Rand uses to describe the parasitical in this work is second-handers. One of the main plot lines of the novel traces the careers of the two architecture students the reader is introduced to in the first few chapters: Peter Keating and Howard Roark. Though Keating possesses a modicum of talent, rather than developing his gift, he guides his life by pursuing what other people think is important. He never learns his craft and when important commissions are called for he puts his name on other people's work. When he achieves everything he thinks he should want, he does not understand the hollowness of it. He will never be satisfied because he has never gone after what he wants. Howard Roark, on the other hand, knows exactly what he wants and is not the least bit interested in what other people think of it. In architectural terms, Roark's work is original. He does not follow an already established school or style. His designs proceed organically from the site, and each building has an intrinsic integrity. As Roark explains to Austen Heller, "Your house is made by its own needs." The architecture produced by second-handers is derivative. John Erik Snyte's firm stocks one architect for each of a number of derivative styles: Classic, Gothic, Renaissance, and even Miscellaneous. Roark is hired because he fits the slot of "Modernistic." What Roark respects is productivity, which he calls competence. He tells Gail Wynand that there is no substitute for it. Not all the love, personality, charity, good feeling in the world will hold up a poorly designed building.

Ability is the touchstone by which all of Roark's friends and Rand's characters are measured. The field does not matter. The social class does not matter. One of Roark's dearest friends is Mike, an electrician he meets on his first construction job. Mike, whose real name is Sean Xavier Donnigan, is passionate about his work, and the people he respects are passionate about theirs: "He worshipped expertness." Once he is convinced about Roark's quality as an architect, he arranges to work on every one of Roark's commissions. All of Roark's other friends, the ones who support him through the trial, are persons of exceptional accomplishment. Steve Mallory, who sculpts the statue of tribute to the human spirit, explains it. When Howard Roark wants to hear what Mallory thinks and not who his family or friends are or about his childhood, the sculptor is overjoyed. He exclaims, "You want to know what I do and why I do it, you want to know what I think?" For Mallory, that means Roark really wants to know what counts about him. They become fast friends. Although Steve has been tried for attempted murder, what counts about him for Roark is his talent as a sculptor.

"First-handers" do not need the approval of others. They know the quality of their own work. Peter Keating needs Ellsworth Toohey to tell him that he is a great architect. Second-handers need committees, unions, and groups to reinforce themselves. There is room in Rand's world for the nonproductive, but only if they are appreciative of the people who create, who produce. In Rand's depiction of contemporary society, this proper relationship has been overturned. Those who are unable to do have made the producers their slaves. In the characterization of employers as evil, the employee has forgotten that without the employer there would be no work. The second-handers of *The Fountainhead* are the moochers and looters of *Atlas Shrugged*. While the second-handers are not productive and litter the cultural world with mediocre works, there is still room in the world of *The Fountainhead* for genuine geniuses to function. In the world of *Atlas Shrugged*, the moochers and looters not only hamper the producers' abilities to function, they pass laws and directives that confiscate not only the means but also the ends of their efforts.

One of John Galt's rationales for the "strike of the Mind" is that if the weak have harnessed the strong to their service (as they claim the strong have exploited the weak in the past), then the strong should use the same means that the weak have used—a strike. When the productive withdraw their talents and abilities, the looter economy crumbles. When there is no host to feed on, a parasite cannot exist. This is the lesson that Rand teaches in *Atlas Shrugged*. In one of Francisco d'Anconia's speeches to Hank Rearden, he explains that Rearden is helping those who torment and hobble him because he still tries to produce with all of their restrictions. Francisco suggests that the only way to defeat looters is by not giving them anything to loot.

Certain motifs recur in Rand's fiction. The flamboyant or extravagant gesture is one. Bjorn Faulkner gives Karen Andre a dress of platinum mesh; "Guts" Regan sends her one pound of orchids; Hank Rearden buys Dagny Taggart an exorbitantly priced pear-shaped ruby to wear for his eyes alone; Dominique Francon secures a priceless sculpture of

Helios from a museum and then destroys it because she considers it too beautiful for a world of second-handers. For Rand's characters, these gestures indicate freedom from monetary and mundane restraints.

Music also plays an important role in Rand's works. It symbolizes the creative and inspirational capacities of humanity. *We the Living* and *Atlas Shrugged* have the strongest musical components. For Kira, "The Song of Broken Glass," a tune from an operetta, encapsulates a sense of the gaiety and joy possible in life. Its promising notes echo in her brain as she dies. Richard Halley's unpublished Fifth Concerto initiates Dagny's search for the great minds that have vanished. Its triumphant strains reverberate in her head through much of the book. As Ayn Rand's body lay in state, light operetta music played as the crowds paid her their last respects.

Trials act as significant plot junctures in the majority of Rand's works of fiction. The most important trial in terms of plot structure is Howard Roark's indictment for blowing up the Cortlandt Housing Project. His acquittal is evidence that justice can prevail and that the individualist does not have to be destroyed. Hank Rearden's trial for defying an unfair government edict also results in his winning. In Rearden's case, he contests the court's jurisdiction over him. In both of these trials, the accused act as their own defense attorneys, and in both, their summation speeches are important statements of Rand's philosophy of personal rights. Since the juries agree with the accused in each case, one could infer that Rand has faith that an average dozen citizens will respond to reason and appreciate greatness. *Night of January 16th* is a courtroom drama; the trial is the plot of this play. There are also trials in *Anthem* and *We the Living*. But whereas the trials in *The Fountainhead* and *Atlas Shrugged* demonstrate the value of the jury system, the trials in the former works are travesties of justice. When Equality 7–2521 will not tell where he has been, he is sent to the Palace of Corrective Detention without a trial. There, on the instruction of two judges, he is lashed repeatedly. Later, his actions and invention are condemned by the ignorance of The World Council of Scholars. When Kira and Leo go to the People's Court to protest the fact that one of their rooms is taken from them, they are judged not on the merits of their case, but upon their ancestry.

Cities, especially those with a skyscraper skyline, are the preferred setting for Rand's stories. Skyscrapers serve as a positive symbol. They represent the potential for human conquest over nature. Rand is not ecology minded. She is enamored of technology and the urban landscape. Kira Argounova's chosen profession is engineering. She keeps a picture of an American skyscraper over her bed. Howard Roark's most important commission is the Wynand Building, which will tower over Hell's Kitchen in New York. When Dagny Taggart walks on the streets of New York, she is filled with reverence by the sight of the skyline.

Rand is the antithesis of a primitivist. Her characters are not refreshed by interaction with nature. For them, nature is there to be harnessed.

The following summaries provide individual overviews of each of Rand's four novels, her one published play, and the one short story published during her lifetime. There is also a summary annotation of *The Early Ayn Rand*, published several years after her death. *We the Living*, *Night of January 16th*, and *Anthem* have been published in revised versions. My discussion derives from the latest editions. There are also anniversary editions of the major novels.

WE THE LIVING (1936)

Begun only four years after the writer arrived in the United States, *We the Living* is, among other things, the fulfillment of a promise Rand made to a guest at the farewell party her family gave for her before she left for America. A man asked her to communicate to Americans that life in Russia was stultifying and that Soviet society was moribund. This may account for its initial title, which was *Airtight*. *We the Living* explicates convincingly the detrimental effects of the Soviet government. The novel is remarkable for a number of reasons, not the least of which is the author's impressive ability to communicate complex and subtle ideological arguments in a newly learned language. Rand explains in the Foreword to the current edition that she did line editing in 1958 to remove some of the awkward construction in the 1936 edition; she also reworded for purposes of clarity. She claims that the revision was minimal. Some readers of both editions have questioned her definition of "minimal." Nonetheless, like Joseph Conrad and Vladimir Nabokov, two other literary giants for whom English was not a native language, she displays an astonishing virtuosity in what was not her native tongue.

Rand comments in the Foreword that *We the Living* is as close to an autobiographical work as she would ever write but that the extent of its resemblance to her life is that she and the heroine hold similar convictions. Although the details of their lives may differ, it is easy to infer from Kira Argounova's story why Rand hated the Marxist system.

The plot of *We the Living* concerns a young woman's struggle to fulfill her capabilities under the frustrating strictures of a Communist regime. Not only is Kira not permitted to complete her engineering studies so she can build the bridges and skyscrapers she has dreamed of constructing, but she is not permitted to leave Russia so that she might follow her dream in another part of the world. Lest any reader misinterpret Rand's message about the effects of the Communist Revolution, through her spokesperson, Kira, Rand makes it clear that the revolution did not fail because it was betrayed (a common argument from those who would indict the particular Soviet system while still embracing the fundamental tenets of communism). Rand explicitly indicts the ideology that fueled the revolution—the supremacy of the collective over the individual. Through the story of Kira and those of other characters, Rand illustrates why such an ideology is detrimental to humanity's capacities for productivity and fulfillment. It glorifies mediocrity, or worse, while stifling the best.

Andrei Taganov is one of the most tragic characters in the book. He is a hero of the revolution, one who sincerely attempts to bring his sisters and brothers up to a humane level of existence. Reacting in good faith to the deprivations he had suffered as a child, he sees communism as a system for the alleviation of the horrors of Czarist Russia. It is only after he experiences the system in action that he begins to realize the magnitude of his miscalculation.

We the Living chronicles the experiences of Kira Argounova, young, bright, and full of enthusiasm for life. The plot begins when her family returns to Petrograd to begin life anew after the revolution. The year is 1922. The family factories have been nationalized, and the Argounova home appropriated for living quarters for a number of families. After a life of luxury, the family must learn to cope with the long lines, shortages, and discrimination against the bourgeoisie that characterize the new regime. Kira becomes a student at the Technological Institute where she meets Andrei Taganov, the hero of Melitopol and other battles of the revolution. Although they are worlds apart ideologically and socially, they are attracted to each other and develop a mutual respect. Eventually, Andrei falls in love with Kira. Although she cares deeply for him, she never returns his love in kind.

Kira, in a pattern duplicated by later Rand heroines, falls in love instantaneously with Leo Kovalensky, whom she meets accidentally on a street in Petrograd. Without knowing anything about him, she is willing to trust her safety to him. Kira and Leo try to escape Russia, but when that fails, they move in together. Although each struggles valiantly to keep the relationship free from pain and drudgery, Leo cannot bring himself to compromise with the system and therefore loses his job. When Leo develops tuberculosis, Kira becomes Andrei's mistress in order to have access to food and money so she can save Leo's life. The situation is ultimately intolerable, and Leo cynically adopts a life of debauchery. Andrei commits suicide, and Kira is killed trying to cross the border.

In the interim, the reader is shown many of the abuses of a totalitarian state and a revolution gone sour as its system is worked to the benefit of "speculators" and plunderers. Rand describes a drab, dull, deadening society. When party membership, rather than ability is the prerequisite for position, progress is undermined and productivity slowed. When individual interests are sacrificed to that vague misnomer "the good of the group," those who would create and contribute color to a society cannot function.

Although it is set specifically in Soviet Russia from 1922 to 1925, and though it details much of what life was like in those post-revolutionary times, *We the Living* is about more than that particular time and place. It is a novel about the individual against the collective, an iconoclastic work for the 1930s when the bulk of *belle-lettres* in America was, if not decidedly leftist, then certainly left-leaning. The worker and the common man and woman became the central figures of much early twentieth-century fiction. For Rand, the common and mediocre were not fit subjects for idealization. Although she expresses faith in the good sense of the average American (her juries usually react rationally), her central characters are exceptional people. She includes characters in her works who are victims, still her protagonists are those who defy the system, who will not give in.

While it does not have the power of *The Fountainhead* or the majestic sweep of *Atlas Shrugged*, *We the Living* is still a compelling story about interesting characters. Its depiction of the day-by-day spirit-destroying activities of life in Russia place it in a group with *One Day in the Life of Ivan Denisovich, Doctor Zhivago*, and other indictments from within and without the pale.

NIGHT OF JANUARY 16TH (1936)

Rand's first professional writing was in the presentational rather than the representational mode. When she was still inexperienced with the language, writing scenarios that others could then flesh out into scripts was a natural starting place. While she was employed by Cecil B. De Mille, she wrote screen scenarios, but as she became more facile in the language, she began to write movie scripts. Her first major sale was the screenplay for an original movie. A good part of her early career was spent in either direct or indirect contact with the movie industry. Her first public success, however, was in the theater.

Called *Penthouse Legend* by its author, produced in Hollywood under the title *Woman on Trial*, Rand's first play opened on Broadway in 1935 with the current title, *Night of January 16th*, and had a successful half-year run.

Night of January 16th is significant for dramatic ingenuity and thematic content. It is because of the latter area that Rand had to continually battle her producer. He wanted to excise the "value" preaching that Rand saw as the determining factor in the jury's ability to judge the heroine's guilt or innocence.

The plot is structured around a trial. All the action takes place in a courtroom. The protagonist, Karen Andre, is accused of murdering Bjorn Faulkner, who was her boss and her lover. There are conflicting stories about whether Faulkner jumped or was pushed from Andre's penthouse ledge.

Bjorn Faulkner had been a free-wheeling, world-class entrepreneur whose financial kingdom was in desperate straits at the time of his death. Two versions of the state of his psyche are presented in court: The prosecution pictures him as a man, reformed by the love of a good woman, who was being blackmailed by his ex-mistress and her gangster lover; the defense contends that Faulkner never changed, that he used himself as collateral so that John Graham Whitfield would extend a ten million dollar loan; his marriage to Nancy Whitfield is a sham.

At the end of Act II, in a dramatic reversal, "Guts" Regan, the gangster and alleged lover of Karen Andre, shows up to announce that Bjorn Faulkner is really dead and that he, Karen, and Bjorn had planned a fake suicide so that Bjorn and Karen could disappear with Whitfield's money. Regan contends and Faulkner's bookkeeper verifies the fact that Whitfield found out about the money being transferred to a bank in Brazil. Regan accuses Whitfield of murdering Faulkner. The jury is left to decide whether a respected banker and his socialite daughter or a secretary-mistress and a gangster in the protection rackets are telling the truth.

Rand called this a "sense of life" play. The characters' actions are meant to be symbolic. Rand got the idea for her plot from the story of the suicide of Ivar Kreugar, a Swede who came to the United States with one hundred dollars and built an international financial empire so vast that he loaned money to nations and controlled half the match industry of the world. After he killed himself, it was discovered that this man, who was imaged in the public mind as "legendary" and "genius," had falsified records and his match kingdom was bankrupt. Whether Kreuger was the victim of bad economic winds or a master criminal was the subject of public debate. Like Icarus, he flew too high and was burned. Rand contends that the press excoriated him, not for his fall, but for his flight. The *New York Times* coverage, however, was generally sympathetic and portrayed Kreugar as a man who was caught in a situation beyond his control, a man whose largesse benefited many countries.

ANTHEM (1938)

If any of Rand's works becomes a staple on high school reading lists, it will be this book. Because of its brevity and parable-like quality, it, like Steinbeck's *The Pearl* or *Of Mice and Men*, communicates to individuals of greatly varying levels of experience and sophistication. One can read it, when young, and assimilate its essential message; the more one lives and works in a world of committees and councils, the more one's recognition is activated by the implications of Rand's portrayal of the possible results when collectivist ideology is taken to its logical extension.

Anthem, like "The Portable Phonograph" or "By the Waters of Babylon," depicts a world after some great war or nuclear holocaust has destroyed all technological advances. In *Anthem*, society has returned to an era of illumination by candlelight. Whereas the world has moved backwards in terms of the benefits of science and technology, the structuring philosophy for the society is the "one world" and "good of the group" ideology that is preached as the goal of so many altruistic political movements of our age. Even the pronoun "I" has been forgotten, and the characters refer to selves as "we." Rand shows us just what it would be like to live for the good of our society rather than ourselves. The picture is not pleasant.

Unlike her other works, in which Rand acts as the omniscient narrator, *Anthem* is narrated by its hero Equality 7–2521, who is twenty-one years old, and because he is taller than and brighter than most of his brothers, he is viewed suspiciously by the elders of his society. Much of the pleasure of the story derives from the use of the readers' imaginations as they fill in the gaps in the hero's knowledge of the Unmentionable Times before the ascendance of the collectivist society. Equality 7–2521 attempts to fight the "evil" in him, which pushes him to learn more and do more than others, but ultimately fails. He commits the Sin of Preference and desires to be sent to the Home of the Scholars, for he has a great thirst for knowledge. The Council of Vocations, however, punishes him and, at the age of fifteen, sentences him to the job of street sweeper for life.

In the course of his drudgery, Equality 7–2521 discovers the remains of an ancient subway and there, using stolen materials, he begins conducting scientific experiments. Although he knows that what he is doing is unlawful in his society, the joy of learning fills his heart, and he keeps his activity a secret. Committing another Sin of Preference, he falls in love with Liberty 5–3000, whom he sees in the fields. She returns his love, and when he must escape the city, she follows him into the Uncharted Forest.

The sin that drives Equality 7–2521 from the society of his brothers is the discovery of electricity, which he would share with the Council of Scholars, but which they reject because it was not a group creation and would threaten the Department of Candles. Like many creators before him, Equality 7–2521 is perceived as a threat to the established order.

Once free of their restrictive society, Equality 7–2521 and Liberty 5–3000 rediscover the knowledge of the Unmentionable Times; they discover the self and free will. Having discovered the "I," they adopt the names Prometheus and Gaea and set about to build a fortress from which they will fight to reclaim the freedom that humanity had lost by its own lack of foresight.

Anthem, which Rand had first thought to title *Ego*, was published in England in 1938, but it was not published in the United States until 1946, when Pamphleteers, which did not generally publish fiction, brought it out in an abridged paperback edition; later Caxton Press issued it in hardback. The New American Library paperback edition has gone through numerous printings. There is even a pulp magazine version that was published in 1953.

THE FOUNTAINHEAD (1943)

Although followers of Ayn Rand's philosophy accept *Atlas Shrugged* as the fullest fictional presentation of her philosophy, from a strictly literary perspective, *The Fountainhead* is a better novel. Both extol the same individualistic virtues, but *The Fountainhead* does so in a more concise and unified manner.

Rand chose the world of contemporary architecture as the setting for her exploration of the difference between beings whose souls are self-actualized and those second-handers whose values are derived, not from any inner urgings, but from what others find valuable. What Rand puts forth in *The Fountainhead* is a rationale for "selfishness" or egoism as a moral good. Architecture is an apt backdrop for Rand's explication because it is simultaneously an art, a science, and a business and, thus, representative of all professions.

Howard Roark, *The Fountainhead*'s protagonist and hero, is an architect. A man of unswerving integrity and exceptional ability, he is guided by no values but his own. The plot follows his career from the day he is expelled from the Architecture School of Stanton Institute of Technology through his difficulties in establishing himself as a working architect to his professional and personal victory and vindication. He diverges from his code on rare occasion and then only in full knowledge of what he is doing.

Juxtaposed against Roark are three other men: Peter Keating, Ellsworth Toohey, and Gail Wynand. Each represents a variation of spiritual collectivism. Gail Wynand, the most tragic figure in *The Fountainhead*, is a cynic who has qualities of greatness, but his disillusionment with his fellow creatures has caused him to seek control over others. Too late, he learns that those whom he thinks he controls actually control him instead. Ellsworth Toohey is as vicious a villain as contemporary literature presents. His goal is power, and he is fully cognizant of the harmful effects of the destructive means he employs toward his ends. By extolling ineptness and mediocrity, Toohey undermines ability and quality; the talentless thereby remain under his influence and the forces that would oppose him are reduced. Peter Keating rises to the top of his profession by manipulating people rather than creating sound architectural designs. Keating is a man whose entire life is ruled by others, to his detriment. The outer trappings of success bring him little lasting satisfaction and eventually he loses even those.

Dominique Francon, Rand's heroine, is an interesting case study in perverseness. She is so convinced of the triumph of evil that she submits herself to every possible degradation lest she chance to hope. She is physically and psychologically masochistic: She is raped by Roark; she marries two men she despises. Dominique's personality, Rand claims, is a representation of herself when she is in a bad mood. Dominique is beautiful and talented. She is desired in different ways by all the main characters, good or evil. When she finally becomes convinced of the error of her ways, she commits herself to becoming Mrs. Howard Roark and sharing his life and happiness.

The novel's climactic scene is a trial at which Howard Roark stands accused of blowing up a housing project that he surreptitiously designed. Peter Keating took credit for the design, but in his contract with Roark, he promised that the plans would not be altered in any way. Roark blows up the project when his contract is not honored and his plans are bastardized beyond recognition. He is exonerated after a thematic speech in which he spells out the significance of the individual creator, who although often damned rather than blessed for his contributions to human progress and happiness, is at the crux of every major human advance. Roark explains that creativity is an individual thing—that the creator works for the joy of the creation, the work being an end in itself. The group may then benefit, but that is a by-product rather than the goal of the creator. He reminds the jury that the United States was created on the principle that the pursuit of happiness is an inalienable right and that that happiness is the happiness of the individual. He spells out the credo he lives by: "I recognize no obligations toward men except one: to respect their freedom and to take no part in a slave society."

Rand's book ends with the triumph of integrity and individualism. She believes that against good, evil is impotent. It is only when the good compromises that it loses its ability to withstand evil. *The Fountainhead* can be read as a modern version of a medieval morality play. Each of its characters represents a variation on the continuum between good and evil. In an age where realism and naturalism reign in character depiction, this seems an anachronism. In twentieth-century fiction, the larger-than-life hero and the unregenerate villain are rare. Although architecture is not the real subject of *The Fountainhead*, the book also reads like a debate among schools of architectural design. Rand did extensive research into the subject and then worked in the office of Eli Jacques Kahn, a famous

New York architect. Her knowledge of architecture is evident throughout the book. Many readers have presumed that the character of Roark was based on Frank Lloyd Wright; however, Rand contends that the only similarity is that both were innovators fighting for modernism as opposed to traditionalism in architecture. Rand is not for parasitism or derivativeness of any kind, so it follows that her hero would design buildings unlike any that had ever been built before.

In *The Fountainhead*, Rand describes the growth of Roark's career by comparing it to a stream that builds below ground, quietly and unobserved, but then bursts forth, bubbling to the surface until it builds into a full torrent. Rand later commented that she did not know that she was also describing the story of her book's popularity. Originally declined by some publishers because they did not think the book would be "commercial," *The Fountainhead* has continued to sell well since its original publication.

ATLAS SHRUGGED (1957)

Atlas Shrugged has been described by more than one critic as "The Bible" of Objectivism. Rand was fond of quoting this novel and on more than one occasion told questioners that if they wanted to know about her philosophy, they need only read *Atlas Shrugged*. The novel has had great appeal, however, to millions who have never heard of Objectivism.

Atlas Shrugged can be read to satisfy any number of tastes. It has been described as a work of science fiction, a mystery story, a female fantasy novel, and a theodicy of capitalism. Regardless of how one approaches it, there is sufficient story to please all but the most praetorian critic. There is adventure, excitement, mystery, romance, surprises, and material enough for mental mastication. It also has the most heroic female protagonist in American fiction: Dagny Taggart.

Dagny runs Taggart Transcontinental Railroad, although her brother, James, is its titular president. He is a weak, indecisive man, given to petty cruelties. In order to keep the railroad functioning properly, she must work around and override him. Her task is complicated by networks of bureaus, councils, and committees and their by-products: lack of responsibility, ineptness, and frustration. The capable seem to be "dropping out." Pride in craftsmanship and earning one's way have become practically nonexistent. At this point, the reader thinks the setting must be here and now and that one is reading a realistic story. It is because of this aspect of the novel that Rand been called prophetic. She is particularly good at describing the failings of collectivist institutions, especially big government.

As things keep breaking down, Dagny sets about to rebuild one of Taggart's old lines, and it is during that task that she contacts Hank

Rearden, a steel tycoon and the inventor of a new kind of metal that is better than steel. They become lovers and battle to keep the economy running, although they must fight even those who claim to be on their side. Ironically, they are fighting their natural allies, other able individualists, who have gone on a "strike of the mind." In fact, Rand's original title for the book was "The Strike."

Three questions plague Dagny: Who is the inventor of an abandoned motor she finds in the ruins of an old factory? Where are all the capable people going? Who is John Galt? The latter is a slang expression that is in general use, conveying a sense of despair. Much of the plot concerns Dagny's attempt to find the answers to these questions.

Her search leads her to discover a utopian community in the mountains of Colorado where the "drop-outs" have set up their free enterprise system. Alternately called Mulligan's Valley or Galt's Gulch, this society serves as a refuge from the looters, scabs, and moochers, who live off the productivity of others while contributing nothing to the society. Born as a reaction against the collectivist maxim "From each according to his ability; to each according to his need," this community's motto is "I swear by my life and my love of it that I will never live for the sake of another man nor ask another man to live for mine."

But Dagny does not stay in the paradisiacal valley; she is not yet ready to leave the world to the looters. Inspired by the vision of Hank Rearden and those like him who still have the courage to fight the moochers, Dagny resolves to try until the end. She returns to a world in shambles. Outbreaks of violence, general despair, a bankrupt economy, and a nation of inept leaders face world crisis.

A national broadcast by Mr. Thompson, the head of state, is announced. As the whole country waits for some reassuring words, the airwaves are commandeered by the men of the mind and in a dissertation-length speech, John Galt spells out the tenets of a rational philosophy: the necessity of choice, the virtue of reason, the importance of independence, the responsibility of judgment. He also explains the causes of the global crisis: mysticism, the concept of original sin, altruism, and what he calls the "cult of zero-worship." He exhorts those remaining to withdraw, to vanish, never to let their strength be used by the weak.

After a melodramatic confrontation during which the desperate looters torture Galt in an attempt to get him to take over and restore the economy, the parasites are finally vanquished. The motor of the world stops, represented by the blackout of the lights of New York City. The strike has succeeded. The productive and creative can return to rebuild.

Atlas Shrugged is a very long and complex novel, and no summary can do justice to its plot and subplots. Francisco d'Anconia and Ragnar Danneskjöld, two of its most fascinating heroic characters, have not been mentioned. The novel also boasts a listing of villainous characters that equals Pope's *Dunciad* for vitreous description and enumeration. Besides the major characters, there are a variety of secondary characters who represent both positive and negative aspects of numerous professions and avocations. Rand's portrait of a crumbling society is an encompassing one.

By the time *Atlas Shrugged* was published, Rand was a well-known author, and a large readership was eagerly awaiting its appearance. It had been fourteen years since the publication of *The Fountainhead*. Although it did not receive a welcome reception by most critics, it has been in print continuously both in hardback and paperback since its original publication.

"THE SIMPLEST THING IN THE WORLD" (1969)

Although it was written in 1940, this short story was not published until twenty-seven years later in *The Objectivist* and then in *The Romantic Manifesto* in 1969. It is the only short story by Rand published in her lifetime. The title is ironic; Henry Dorn, the protagonist, is trying to convince himself that the simplest thing in the world would be to write formula fiction. However, for a man of his creative abilities, it is anything but simple to force his mind into mundane patterns. Most of the story takes place in his mind as he battles his natural inclinations and tries to force himself to write for the commercial market. As Rand explained in the headnote, "The story illustrates the nature of the creative process—the way in which an artist's sense of life directs the integrating functions of his subconscious and controls his creative imagination."

THE EARLY AYN RAND: A SELECTION FROM HER UNPUBLISHED FICTION (1984)

This posthumously published anthology is divided chronologically. The first part is composed of four short stories, written from 1926 to 1929. The second and third parts, written during the thirties, include unpublished excerpts from *We the Living* and *The Fountainhead*, a movie synopsis, and two plays.

Part I begins with the melodramatic "The Husband I Bought." Its heroine, like Kira Argounova, sacrifices herself for a man unable to appreciate her worth. A more sympathetic interpretation is that Irene, the heroine, is one not willing to settle for less than the ideal, and therefore, her action is self-preservation, not self-sacrifice. The next two stories, "Good Copy" and "Escort," are in a more light-hearted vein, particularly illuminating for what they show us of Rand's early experiments with varying tones. In them, her satire is light, her use of irony reflective of her appreciation for O. Henry. Laury McGee, the male protagonist of "Good Copy," is a reporter who stages a kidnapping in order to create an exciting story, the "good copy" of the title. The plot line prefigures such recent films as *A Life Less Ordinary* and *Excess Baggage*, in which the kidnapped directs her own kidnapping. "Escort" is reminiscent of O. Henry's "The Gift of the Magi." In it, the wife scrimps and saves to put together enough money to buy an "escort" for one night of gaiety, the irony being that her husband is working as just such an escort in order to support them. "Her Second Career" is darker in tone, satirizing Hollywood and the vagaries of fame.

"Red Pawn" has many of the plot patterns of *We the Living*. This is not surprising since they were written during the same time period, the early thirties. Like the novel, it takes place in Soviet Russia. Both heroines become mistresses to Communist heroes in order to save the men they love. Joan is successful where Kira Argounova was not. Like Charles Darnay, in Dickens's *A Tale of Two Cities*, Kareyev, the prison commandant known as "The Beast," goes to his certain death by assuming the identity of Michael, the husband of the woman he loves. "Red Pawn" was originally sold in 1932 to Universal Pictures for $1,500. It was later traded to Paramount Pictures for a property that cost Paramount $20,000. It was never produced.

Ideal has been produced, though not in Rand's lifetime. Michael Paxton, who masterminded the Academy Award-nominated biographical documentary *Ayn Rand: A Sense of Life*, had previously directed *Ideal* in a little theater venue in Los Angeles in 1989.[1] Its plot involves a Garbo-inspired movie actress searching for integrity in the fans that claim to worship her. Only one, ironically a friendless bum, proves himself no hypocrite.

"Think Twice" is a dramatization of Rand's contempt for the do-gooders of this earth. Its villain, Walter Breckenridge, uses his charity to control and keep dependent those that he claims to be helping. When he is murdered, there are any number of the beneficiaries of his charity who could have happily done the deed. The play has enough irony and plot twists to satisfy the most avid murder mystery fan.

Completing the sampling of *The Early Ayn Rand* are two significant excerpts cut from the final version of *The Fountainhead*. "Vesta Dunning" is the story of Howard Roark's first romantic liaison. Vesta, like a number of Rand's female characters, is an actress. She has an unusual presence and talent—a young Katharine Hepburn comes to mind—but she compromises her integrity in the service of her final goal. Changing her name to Sally Ann Blainey, she becomes a star, the first woman "to make strength attractive on the screen." The other excerpt contains scenes between Roark and Cameron in which the characterization of Roark is not always in keeping with his final realization in the novel.

Reading *The Early Ayn Rand* is a pleasurable experience. One runs across startling, fresh imagery; a particular favorite is the description of Claire Nash's eyes as "soft violets hidden among pine needles of mascara." Rand's incipient sensuousness is evidenced in her description of the feel of satin, the glimmer of crystal, the reflective glow of red wine. Even in the earliest stages of her development in craft and language, Rand's nascent virtuosity is evident.

JOURNALS OF AYN RAND (1997)

This collection includes samples of Rand's fiction and nonfiction. Returning to early samples of Rand's development as a writer, it includes a scenario for the silent screen that she wrote for Cecil B. De Mille. Called "The Skyscaper," her notes detail the process of her adaptation of a story of the same name written by Dudley Murphy. Her writing alternates between English and Russian (translated for the reader). When De Mille produced the movie in 1928, he did not use Rand's scenario. A second scenario, "The Siege," and her first attempt at a novel, "The Little Street," are also part of the chapter on Rand's earliest writings in the United States. As the editor of the *Journals* notes: "It is fascinating to see the seeds of her later work in these stories."

Unfortunately, a number of Rand's unproduced screenplays have been lost or misplaced, but the Rand estate has promised publication of such works as *Love Letters* and *You Came Along*, which were filmed. Fortunately, Rand's notes for an original screenplay on the development of the atomic bomb, "Top Secret," are included in the *Journals*. Of particular interest to creative writers are the extensive notes that detail the analytical gestation process that undergirded Rand's creation of plot, character, and theme.

NOTE

1. The program heralds it as "The World Premier." The Melrose Theatre was the host for this Keller Enterprises production, which ran Thursdays through Sundays from 13 October to 19 November 1989.

CHAPTER 3

A Compendium of Characters

Character may be the most significant element in Ayn Rand's fiction. To her, literary personages are of such importance that she found the image of one, Enjolras, the brave, passionate defender of right and liberty in Victor Hugo's *Les Miserables*, sufficient to sustain her when she faced the possibility of death as a young girl in revolutionary Russia. Part of her credo of literature is that the writer of fiction should populate her stories with individuals who inspire us, ideal characters, people we would want to meet, rather than characters like the people next door. Over and over again, in her writing career, she resisted the direction of movie studio editors or publishing house executives who enjoined her to write about "realistic people," people she might meet on the street. What has been depicted by critics as her "stylized vice-and-virtue character(s)" is not a fault, but results from a conscious literary decision.

The purpose of this chapter, then, is to provide an index to those virtuous and villainous fictional characters who symbolize the ideal and the evil in humanity. Most of Rand's characters fall neatly into one or the other of those categories, although there are a few crossover or neutral characters. For the sake of organization, I have classified Rand's significant fictional characters into six categories: (1) the heroic protagonists, (2) other primary heroic personages, (3) lesser characters of virtue, (4) the archvillainous antagonists, (5) secondary unworthy or villainous characters, and (6) neutral or metamorphosing characters. The characters will be organized according to the literary work in which they appear. Within each work, the characters will be arranged alphabetically. I have not included characters from fiction published after Rand's death.

THE HEROIC PROTAGONISTS

Rand's protagonists share many traits. They are all Romantic rebels against restrictive and mundane societies. In their rebellion, they act alone and on principle. Although, in some cases, they may be joined by the like-minded, that factor is never crucial to their revolt. They are all intellectually gifted and have unusual talents. The modern literary term for the main character is protagonist, which means the chief striver, rather than hero. The protagonist is the character whose struggle or story is the main focus of the plot. This term is appropriate in modern fiction because many of the main characters in contemporary literature are anything but heroic. In Rand's case, however, the traditional terminology would be applicable. All her protagonists are also heroes.

We the Living (1936)

Kira Alexandrovna Argounova   Kira Argounova is the closest to an autobiographical character that Rand creates. Although Rand claims that Kira is autobiographical only in that they share beliefs, there are also some details of their lives that are parallel. Both are young students at the time of the Russian revolution. Both are daughters of prosperous businessmen whose businesses were nationalized by the Communist government. Kira is described as slender and proud, with a defiant posture; pictures of the young Ayn Rand show a similar woman. As a young girl, Kira is inspired by the character of a Viking in a story; Ayn Rand's literary hero was Cyrus, a brave, arrogant, and daring British officer in a children's story. Rand's first love was named Leo. Unwilling to adjust to the Communist regime, Ayn Rand received a passport to leave Russia in 1925; Kira Argounova, whose passport application is refused, is killed trying to cross the Latvian border. Kira is young, eighteen when the novel begins, gray eyed, with brown hair, and a determination not to let the collectivist system wear her down. She wants to be an engineer and build steel structures; the only career, other than writing, that Rand considered was engineering. Kira rejects religion and treacly fairy tales, and once she has encountered the man she loves, Leo Kovalensky, she is willing to do anything to secure his health and well-being. Unmindful of her material surroundings, she wants only to be allowed to fulfill the best that is in her.

Night of January 16th (1936)

Karen Andre   A proud, defiant animal underlies the cool, calm, detached persona that Karen Andre projects on the witness stand. Slender and elegant, Karen wears her simple, tailored clothes with the authority of timeless fashion. The prosecution witnesses characterize her as shameless and pagan, a primitive seductress who would rather kill the man she loves than allow him to be happy with another woman. The defense portrays her as a capable, loyal, passionately-in-love woman who is willing to do anything, including forgery and fraud, to aid her lover, Bjorn Faulkner. Karen and Bjorn are lovers and business associates from the first day he hires her as his secretary. Karen is twenty-eight at the time of the trial. Her fate is decided by a jury made up of twelve members of the audience. Rand, obviously, declares her to be "not guilty."

Anthem (1938)

Equality 7–2521   Six feet tall, twenty-one years old, and equipped with a quick and inquisitive mind in a futuristic society that values only sameness, Equality 7–2521 must forge a difficult path to identity. Defying the edicts of his brothers, he experiments with electicity to become the literal and figurative bringer of light, like Prometheus, whose name he eventually takes. The woman he loves, Liberty 5–3000, thinks of him as "The Unconquered" and together they escape their collectivist society to build a fort of individualism from which he and his chosen friends can begin their battle for freedom, rights, and honor.

The Fountainhead (1943)

Howard Roark   When the novel begins, Howard Roark is a young architecture student. He is encountered naked and laughing, an innocent Adam, poised on a cliff. Roark's looks have comic-strip color and clarity: orange hair and gray eyes, a contemptuous mouth, a sure and self-sufficient attitude. He cares nothing about what other people think of him. The quality he demands in his friends is a "self-sufficient ego." He does not see a love relationship as an amalgamation of beings. He believes that in order to say "I love you," one must first be an "I." Roark is a brilliant architect, unwilling to compromise the integrity of his creations for the sake of monetary gains. The only compromises Roark makes are for either Dominique Francon, the woman he loves, or Gail Wynand, his friend. In these cases, he is true to himself, for they are people he values. He is, in Peter Keating's words, "the most egotistical and the kindest man." Consistent to the end, he is able to convince a jury of the validity of his position after he blows up a housing project for the poor. His plan for the project was altered, contrary to his contract. After his exoneration, Gail Wynand contracts with him to build the tallest skyscraper in New York City, the Wynand Building, even though

Wynand has lost his wife, Dominique, to Roark and his newspaper, the *Banner*, in fighting Roark's cause. The building is to be a tribute to Roark's spirit.

Atlas Shrugged (1957)

Dagny Taggart   Dagny Taggart is probably the most admirable and successful heroine in American fiction. Not only is her worth acclaimed by her allies, but even her enemies acknowledge her extraordinary abilities. As vice-president in charge of operation, she runs Taggart Transcontinental, the largest railroad in the country, although her brother James Taggart is the titular head. In her early thirties, young looking, slender, with shapely legs and medium-length brown hair, she does not look the part of a railroad tycoon. Her authority derives from her ability. Her first lover is Francisco d'Anconia, but his inexplicable transition into a playboy leaves her hurt and dismayed. She accepts the challenge of rebuilding the Rio Norte Line (which she renames the John Galt Line) and in the process develops a relationship with Hank Rearden, who helps fund the line. Although he is married, she becomes his mistress. Together they try to keep the national economy from falling apart. Dagny fights longer than any of the people of accomplishment against giving the world over to the moochers and looters. Even after she meets and falls in love with John Galt and understands the nature of his strike, she will not give up her railroad. At the conclusion of the novel, Dagny and John Galt, along with the other people of the mind, are ready to return and rebuild.

"The Simplest Thing in the World" (1969)

Henry Dorn   Henry Dorn is the author of a book called *Triumph*, which was anything but what its name suggests. The critics had either disliked or misunderstood it. As his wife Kitty plays solitaire, Dorn sits at his desk trying to write a simple story, one the public would like. But each story he concocts in his mind takes his imagination on flights of philosophical fancy, and he knows that what may be the simplest thing in the world for people without integrity is impossible for him.

OTHER PRIMARY HEROIC PERSONAGES

The following characters are often of equal stature with the protagonist in that they either embody equivalent values or are adjuncts in the quest to maintain or discover the good.

We the Living (1936)

Leo Kovalensky   Although he is not an ideal male, Leo Kovalensky is the prototype for later Rand heroes. Like other Rand protagonists, he has haughty eyes, a contemptuous smile, and looks as if he were born to carry a whip. Described as handsome enough to model for a bust of Apollo, straight, tall, and proud, even in his penurious state, Leo succumbs to cynicism and becomes a gigolo, hell-bent for destruction. Leo serves as an example of how the injustices of collectivism destroy the fine and the able. Although Kira Argounova adores Leo as the embodiment of her highest values, he turns out to be unworthy of her sacrifices on his behalf.

Andrei Taganov   One of Rand's most sympathetic, misguided, but worthy characters, Andrei Taganov is a Communist, a fearless soldier, a heroic revolutionary, battle-scarred, with the look of a tamed tiger. Andrei's difficult childhood leads him naturally into revolution against a system that has oppressed him and his family. Ascetic, and passionately devoted to bringing the masses up to his level, he learns the full extent of the party's corruption only in the course of his G.P.U. (secret police) work. Although he has been betrayed by Kira, he understands her reasons and continues to help her. His integrity will not allow him to remain silent about the betrayal of the revolution, and he comes to realize that even its ideals were not valid.

Night of January 16th (1936)

Bjorn Faulkner   Although he never appears in the play, Bjorn Faulkner's character is the focus of the plot. He is strong and audacious. Other men's rules do not hamper him. He is willing to swindle, forge, and even sell himself as security for his financial empire. A man who takes what he wants, he also gives generously. He is a man of flamboyant gestures; he gives Karen Andre a fine platinum mesh gown, which when heated and slipped on her, has a more erotic effect than nudity. The audience is asked to judge if such a man could change his ways and settle down with a socialite wife or if, to the end, he would remain a man of such self-esteem, of such overweening spirit, that he would not be conquered except by death. Rand based his character on Ivar Kreugar, the Swedish "Match King" who committed suicide when his empire collapsed in 1932.

Larry "Guts" Regan   Tall and slender, with light eyes and an assured manner, Larry "Guts" Regan is a notorious outlaw whose main enterprise is running a protection racket. Because of his love for Karen, which is the one good and true thing that ever happened to him, "Guts" is willing to participate in the fake suicide of Bjorn Faulkner. He even procures the body of a murdered gunman to substitute for Faulkner's body. He is accused by the district attorney of helping Karen to murder Bjorn, although he claims that John Whitfield is the real culprit and paid him $5,000 to keep quiet about discovering Whitfield's car near the field that Faulkner was to use for his getaway.

Anthem (1938)

Liberty 5–3000   Seventeen, straight, and "thin as a blade of iron," Liberty 5–3000 is thought of by Equality 7–2521 as "The Golden One." Her eyes are dark and project a hard, glowing, and fearless quality. She knows no guilt. She is brave and single-minded, for she goes alone into the Uncharted Forest to follow Equality 7–2521. She takes the name of Gaea, for she will give birth to a new breed of godlike humans.

The Fountainhead (1943)

Dominique Francon   Dominique Francon is a beautiful woman, with a body so exquisite that she models for a statue of tribute to the indomitable human spirit. Dominique's fragile appearance, pale gold hair, and gray eyes belie a capable, cynical, and disarmingly blunt manner. Proceeding from the conviction that good has no chance in this world, a premise that is the opposite of Rand's belief, Dominique chooses not to care about anything in order not to let anything or anyone have power over her. Rand has characterized Dominique as "myself in a bad mood." Masochistic in the extreme, Dominique marries men she despises in order to prove to herself that she does not care. She has a strong perverse streak—she tries to destroy Howard Roark, the man she loves, because she hopes she will not be able to do so. Whenever she does something particularly hurtful to him, she goes to him and sleeps with him. Her marriage to Peter Keating is ended by Gail Wynand, who buys Dominique from Peter for $250,000 and the Stoneridge commission. Although Dominique begins the marriage to Wynand as an expression of self-contempt, she learns to care for him. Only when Gail Wynand, in order to save the *Banner*, gives up his battle to protect Roark, does Dominique, openly and in a scandalous manner, give Wynand reason to divorce her. By the end of the novel, Dominique has learned to accept happiness and live openly and unafraid as Mrs. Howard Roark.

Gail Wynand   Gail Wynand is one of Rand's most tragic characters. As a young boy, he pulls himself out of the miserable environment of Hell's Kitchen in search of beauty and integrity. His quest brings disillusionment and cynicism, and in his bitterness, he looks for people of quality and integrity only in order to break them. He surrenders himself to the vulgar and the mediocre, turning his newspaper, the *Banner*, into a cheap scandal sheet, full of crime and sentiment. He is described by Austen Heller as "an exquisite bastard." Paying with his honor for unlimited power leaves him with nothing more to conquer; bored and in a state of misanthropy, he is ready to play Russian roulette. The statue of Dominique Francon renews his interest in life. Unfortunately, Wynand meets Dominique and Howard Roark too late. Having given himself over to second-handers, he cannot use his newspaper effectively when he decides to battle for positive values. Although he fights valiantly to save Roark, in the end he capitulates and then cannot forgive himself. He divorces Dominique, closes down the *Banner*, but does give Roark the Wynand Building commission, which includes a proviso that he and Howard are never to meet again.

Atlas Shrugged (1957)

Francisco d'Anconia   Born to aristocracy and wealth, Francisco d'Anconia begins in his youth to develop his considerable natural abilities. Every d'Anconia, since the first ancestor fled the Inquisition, by tradition must earn the right to the name and leave the family fortune larger than when he received it. A man with great *joi de vivre*, he looks the part of nobility. Tall, slender, dark-haired and blue-eyed, he carries himself with style, as if a cape were unfurling behind him. While still in college, he works his way from furnace boy to factory owner, and by the age of twenty-three, he is the copper king of the world. Then inexplicably, he changes. At thirty-six, he has the reputation of a dissipated playboy. Francisco is Dagny Taggart's first love, and later, he becomes Hank Rearden's friend. His is the job of reeducating Rearden; to that end, he delivers several of the most important theoretical speeches in the novel: the oration that contains the title imagery and the renunciation of the "money is the root of all evil" concept. He tries to convince both Hank and Dagny to stop placing their abilities at the service of second-raters. Francisco pays the highest price for his ideals: He loses Dagny first to Rearden and then to John Galt; he destroys the d'Anconia mines. Nevertheless, Francisco's strength of character and devotion to his ideals make him capable of absorbing all the losses and still reaping joy out of his existence.

Ragnar Danneskjöld   One of the triumverate that sets out to stop the motor of the world, Ragnar Danneskjöld, scion of European aristocracy, first meets his lifelong friends, Francisco d'Anconia and John Galt, when they are freshmen at Patrick Henry University. Ragnar is an incredibly beautiful man with hair of gold and the audacity of a buccaneer.

A gentle and delicate intellectual, Ragnar studies philosophy, but he becomes an international pirate, sinking ships laden with foreign aid or important raw materials. He blows up Orren Boyle's furnances to prevent Boyle from manufacturing the ill-gotten formula for Rearden Metal. One of his goals is to destroy the myth of Robin Hood. Rather than steal from the rich and give to the poor, he steals from the undeserving and gives to the deserving. Danneskjöld's part in the novel is not as large as that of d'Anconia, Galt, or Hank Rearden, but as an ideal, he completes the picture of how men of ability and integrity must respond to a world of moochers and looters. He is married to Kay Ludlow, an actress, and their marriage is an illustration of a relationship of equals.

John Galt   The ideal hero or code hero of *Atlas Shrugged*, John Galt is the man who stops the motor of the world when he leads the men of the mind on strike against all the leeches and parasites they have been sustaining throughout history. It is Galt who, as a young engineer at Twentieth Century Motors, revolts against the collectivist credo and says, "I will put an end to this, once and for all." Self-made and self-educated, John Galt leaves his home somewhere in Ohio and, as a student, is the most promising young physicist to ever matriculate at Patrick Henry University. He calls his friends, Francisco d'Anconia and Ragnar Danneskjöld, to join him and become flame-spotters, who find flares of genius and convince other productive individuals to join them in their strike. Hard and gaunt, with chestnut-brown hair and deep, dark green eyes, Galt's suntanned body and guilt-free face inspire instant recognition and respect from Dagny Taggart. As an unknown worker for Taggart Transcontinental, he wins Eddie Willer's trust and undermines Dagny's efforts to keep capable people working. Galt does not appear, except in disguise, until halfway through the novel. He is, however, Rand's spokesperson, and in his challenge to the villains to relinquish their hold on the government, he delivers a sixty-page speech, which is the philosophical crux of the story. Ironically, Dagny has thought of Galt as "the destroyer" when in actuality he is the builder of Mulligan's Valley, an ideal community in the mountains of Colorado, and the leader into a free and productive world to come. He is the culmination of Rand's effort to portray the ideal man.

Hank Rearden   A man of little self-understanding, Hank Rearden is an industrialist of tremendous ability, an inventor who perfects Rearden Metal, an alloy stronger and more flexible than steel. He shows little overt emotion; tall and gaunt, with ice-blue eyes and ash blond hair, his appearance is strong but expressionless. A perfectionist, he looks for fault in himself, unable to understand the attitudes of those who claim they love him. He marries Lillian because he thinks she is someone to attain, and when she is frigid, he convinces himself that his desires are depraved. He does not understand the nature of his passion for Dagny Taggart, initially, because he is one who is convinced of the mind/body dichotomy. He showers her with lavish gifts: a pear-shaped ruby, a blue fox cape, gold bracelets, and fine crystal. His guilt about his love for Dagny permits Lillian to manipulate him and cripples his ability to judge others. However, he soon becomes more self-aware and begins to rebel against his self-imposed martyrdom. In his refusal to recognize the court's right to dispose of his property without his consent, he delivers a consummate defense of capitalism. Although his feelings for Francisco d'Anconia are strained by Francisco's superficial public image, their friendship grows until Rearden finds out that Francisco had been Dagny's lover. Once he learns about Mulligan's Valley and becomes one of the strikers, he is among people who appreciate his value and who will be friends worthy of him.

LESSER CHARACTERS OF VIRTUE

Minor characters serve to reinforce Rand's themes. Although these characters do not always play significant roles in the plot, they do serve to exemplify certain virtues and/or to give aid and succor to the protagonists.

We the Living

Sasha Chernov   Sasha Chernov is a young student of history who is thrown out of the University because of his background and political views. He is Irina Dunaev's fiancé, and his counterrevolutionary activity earns him exile to Siberia.

Irina Dunaev   Irina Dunaev is a talented artist with a bent for satiric drawings. She is naturally loving and does not accept conventional values; therefore, she is the only one in her family who visits Kira Argounova when the rest reject her as a fallen woman. Her "sanctity of life" speech when she is about to be shipped off to sure death in Siberia is one of the keynotes of the novel.

Vasili Ivanovitch Dunaev   Once a tall, powerful man of some community stature, Vasili Ivanovitch Dunaev becomes stooped and self-deluding about the future of the Communist regime. He keeps expecting Europe to intervene. Vasili is a man of great spirit and principle; he refuses to get a Soviet job or adjust to the new order. Although he tries to rationalize the behavior of his son Victor Dunaev, he eventually disowns Victor when he realizes the full extent of his perfidy.

Glieb Ilyitch Lavrov   Father of Marisha Lavrov, Glieb Ilyitch Lavrov is a man of the working class who spent years exiled in Siberia for fighting Czarist oppression. He refuses to be co-opted by the Soviet regime and denounces it as heartily as he denounced the Czar.

Stepan Timonshenko   Stepan Timonshenko is a hard, tough sailor in the Red Baltic fleet. However, he does not lack sensitivity. When he realizes the situation of Kira Argounova and Leo Kovalensky, he helps Kira get away and frees Leo from jail. A good friend to Andrei Taganov, and a dedicated revolutionary, he realizes early that the revolution has been perverted and that gluttonous speculators and opportunists will profit rather than the masses he fought to free. His last act is to try to protect Andrei; he sends him a letter that will safeguard him from Pavel Syerov.

Night of January 16th

Defense Attorney Stevens   A man who projects sophistication and urbane gentility, Stevens does an admirable job defending Karen Andre. In his closing argument, he captures the essence of the opposing senses of life that are dramatized in the persons of Bjorn Faulkner and John Whitfield.

Siegurd Jungquist   Bjorn Faulkner's loyal bookkeeper, turned secretary, Siegurd Jungquist has unswerving admiration for his boss. Although his devotion to Faulkner and Karen is evident, he is not a good witness for them because he proudly acknowledges that he would lie for Faulkner. He is probably the inadvertent cause of Faulkner's murder when he reveals information to Whitfield about the whereabouts of the ten million dollars Faulkner transferred to Buenos Aires.

Anthem

International 4–8818   Tall, strong, with a sense of humor and a tendency to smile in a society where such behavior is not encouraged, International 4–8818 maintains an unspoken friendship with Equality 7–2521. It is a show of preference, which is a sin in their brotherhood. International 4–8818 keeps his friend's secret and does not report Equality 7–2521's crime against the Council.

The Fountainhead

Henry Cameron   Henry Cameron is a cantankerous, overbearing old man who has been at the top of the field of architecture. Because he did not pay his dues to society, he is reduced to a ramshackle office and few commissions. Still passionate about his work, though drink has made some inroads on his health, he allows Howard Roark to work for him.

He is fearful, however, of what the powers-that-be will do to Roark's integrity. His philosophy of architecture is that no building should copy any other.

Roger Enright   Roger Enright is a self-made man who owns numerous businesses outright. He started his life as a coal miner and made his way to the top in a singlehanded manner. Enright hires Howard Roark as the architect for The Enright House, which Dominique Francon characterizes as the most beautiful building in New York.

John Fargo   Because he admires both Jimmy Gowan's Service Station and Austen Heller's house, John Fargo asks Howard Roark to design the Fargo store, which will be built on the location of a former competitor's store.

Jimmy Gowan   A man who has worked like a mule to raise enough money to build his own business, Jimmy Gowan hires Roark to build his gas station. He does not care what people think.

Austen Heller   The man who gives Howard Roark his start by giving Roark $500 to open an office and a contract to build his house, Austen Heller remains Roark's friend and supporter throughout Roark's career. Heller, a tall, broad-shouldered, square-faced man with sandy hair and calm eyes, is a writer of national stature and following, the star columnist for the *Chronicle*. In several instances he writes articles in defense of Roark; he does so during both of Roark's court cases. Heller also tries to send Roark clients and is responsible for the article that makes Roark famous. He acts as a self-appointed guardian, always warning Roark and watching out for him, although, more often than not, Roark does not listen.

Kent Lansing   Kent Lansing comes into Roark's life out of the blue and gets Roark a commission to build the Aquitania, a luxurious hotel on Central Park South. Lansing is a man of integrity who knows quality and will fight to have what he wants. He understands the psychology of boards and unions and corporations, which he equates with "other chain gangs," and because he knows what he wants while others do not, he gets what he wants.

Steven Mallory   A sculptor of heroic figures, Steven Mallory has been so buffeted by life that he is reduced to creating plaster baby plaques for dime stores. Mallory is, at first, too bitter to believe that Roark wants him to create a sculpture for the Stoddard Temple for no reason other than the quality of his work. Mallory tries to kill Ellsworth Toohey, and although he will not disclose the reason in court, he later explains to Roark the nature of Toohey's treachery. Roark and Mallory become friends, and Mallory becomes an unknowing intermediary in the relationship between Howard and Dominique. Mallory is passionate, high-strung, and an artist of great ability; his talent is immediately appreciated by Roark, Toohey, and Gail Wynand. His nude statue of Dominique, in an attitude of exaltation, representing the heroic human spirit, is the centerpiece for the Stoddard Temple.

Atlas Shrugged

In *Atlas Shrugged*, most of the able and virtuous people join the strike of the mind and become deserters. Some live on the outside, doing menial jobs, thereby not allowing the moochers and the leeches to utilize their brain power. Some move into Mulligan's Valley on a full-time basis. A few in this list are good people who have not found their way to the strikers, but find themselves unable to function in the collectivist and bureaucratic society.

Hugh Akston   A philosophy professor at Patrick Henry University who functions as a father figure for Francisco d'Anconia, Ragnar Danneskjöld, and John Galt, Hugh Akston is one of the last advocates of reason in the halls of academe, a believer that contradictions do not exist. He quits academia and works in a diner when he is not in the valley.

Jeff Allen   A skilled lathe operator who cannot find an honest job and therefore becomes a bum, Jeff Allen is put in charge of a stranded train by Dagny Taggart. He tells Dagny the story of Twentieth Century Motor Company.

Calvin Atwood   The owner of Atwood Light and Power Company of New York City, Calvin Atwood becomes the owner of Atwood Leather Goods Company in Mulligan's Valley.

Bill Brent   The chief dispatcher for the Colorado Division of Taggart Transcontinental, Bill Brent warns David Mitchum about the possible tunnel disaster, refuses to sign the order to send the Comet through the tunnel, and quits rather than be forced to do what he knows is wrong.

Tom Colby   The rolling mill foreman and head of the Rearden Steel Workers Union, a company union, Tom Colby quits when Directive 10–289 is declared.

Dan Conway   A square and solid man near fifty who runs the Phoenix/Durango railroad, Dan Conway is Taggart Transcontinental's chief competitor in Colorado until the Anti–dog-eat-dog Rule is declared. Then he retires to his ranch in Arizona.

Ken Danagger   The owner of Danagger Coal in Pennsylvania, Ken Danagger started as a miner. In his fifties at the time of the collectivist takeover, he tries to help Hank Rearden and is indicted with him for subverting government orders. Although he loves his work and his mines, he retires and leaves the mines to no one.

Quentin Daniels   Quentin Daniels is a young physicist who has refused to work for Dr. Stadler at the State Science Institute but agrees to try to help Dagny reconstruct the motor. He resigns his job with her because he does not want the motor to be used in the service of tyranny. It is when she is trying to keep him from disappearing that Dagny crashes into the valley.

Richard Halley   The composer whose heroic music is the theme song for the novel, Richard Halley is a composer of intrepid, rebellious, and inspirational music. He achieves acclaim after many years of struggle but retires the day after the success of his opera, *Phaethon*.

Lawrence Hammond   The last producer of good cars and trucks in the outer world, Lawrence Hammond, the owner of Hammond Car Company in Colorado, retires to run the grocery store in Mulligan's Valley.

Mrs. William Hasting   The widow of the man who was chief engineer of the laboratory at Twentieth Century Motors, Mrs. Hasting is a dignified and serene woman who gives Dagny the clue that leads to Hugh Akston.

Dr. Thomas Hendricks   A great surgeon who retires and vanishes after the socialization of medicine, Dr. Thomas Hendricks treats Dagny after her crash into Mulligan's Valley.

Gwen Ives   Hank Rearden's calm and efficient secretary, Gwen Ives breaks down in tears when she hears of the passing of the Equalization of Opportunity Bill.

Owen Kellog   The first drop-out that Dagny Taggart encounters, Owen Kellog is a young engineer who was assistant to the manager of Taggart Terminal in New York. He refuses her offer of a promotion. They meet on the frozen train and then again in Mulligan's Valley.

Pat Logan   The engineer of the Taggart Comet on the Nebraska Division, Pat Logan wins the lottery to drive the first run of the John Galt Line on the rails of Rearden Metal.

Kay Ludlow   Kay Ludlow is an unusual beauty who was a movie star. She is married to Ragnar Danneskjöld and waits in the valley while Ragnar risks his life. She performs plays there by authors unknown to the outside world.

Roger Marsh   Roger Marsh has owned a factory of electrical appliances near the town of Marshville. He tries not to desert but eventually does without leaving a word for Ted Nielsen. He grows cabbage in Mulligan's Valley.

Ray McKim   A large, grinning, and confident young fireman, Ray McKim works the first run of the John Galt Line.

Dick McNamara   Among the best contractors in the country, Dick McNamara is one of the first of Dagny's business associates to walk out. He quits with a pile of contracts and a three-year waiting list of clients.

Michael "Midas" Mulligan   Although he looks like a truck driver, Michael "Midas" Mulligan is the richest man in the country, a banker. He owns the valley where all the able and competent have gathered to build their own Atlantis and await the downfall of the collectivist state. The valley bears his name, and he runs a bank there where all exchange is done in gold.

Judge Narragansett   Once the judge of the Superior Court of Illinois, Judge Narragansett runs a chicken and dairy farm in Mulligan's Valley. He quit the bench when a court of appeals reversed his ruling that those who earn are more entitled than those whose only claim is need. He would not uphold injustice.

Ted Nielsen   Ted Nielsen, the owner of Nielsen Motors, quits and disappears when the John Galt Line is closed. In Mulligan's Valley he works as a lumberjack.

Dwight Sanders   A maker of good airplanes, Dwight Sanders, who owned Sanders Aircraft, becomes a hog farmer and plane attendant in Mulligan's Valley.

Andrew Stockton   One of the people whose profession does not change in the valley, Andrew Stockton has the Stockton Foundry there as he had it in Stockton, Colorado. Stockton is an eager competitor who is anxious to hire the sort of people who might one day be his most able competition.

Mr. Ward   Mr. Ward is the fourth generation of his family to run Ward Harvester Company in Minnesota. It is a small, solid company, and Mr. Ward is ready to sell at a loss if it means keeping his doors open. He comes to Hank Rearden because he cannot get steel, and Rearden gets it for him.

Ellis Wyatt   Young, quick-tempered, and able, Ellis Wyatt is in the business of reviving old oil wells and making them produce again. A loner, he invites Dagny and Hank to dinner and to spend the night at his home at the conclusion of the first run of the John Galt Line. After the crippling directives are issued, he destroys Wyatt Oil and vanishes into Mulligan's Valley.

THE ARCHVILLAINOUS ANTAGONISTS

Just as Rand's goal in writing Romantic fiction is to portray the ideal man and thereby accomplish the didactic purpose of illustrating desirable human behavior, so she parallels the lesson by illustrating through her antagonists and villains those kinds of peoples and behaviors that are most repulsive and detrimental to human happiness. She creates two types of negative characters: Those who are weak or ignorant and thereby impede their own and the progress of others, and those who choose to do evil. In this category of the archvillainous antagonists, I have included only characters of the latter type. The archvillains are individuals who seek power, a power they use to do ill, even ultimately to themselves.

We the Living

Victor Dunaev   An opportunist of the first order, Victor Dunaev has no loyalty or honor. He uses everyone. He marries Marisha Lavrova because he thinks her proletariat background will help him in the party. When that is not enough to get him the job he wants, he turns in his sister Irina and her fiancé Sasha Chernov for counterrevolutionary activities to prove his loyalty to the party. Although he looks like a matinee idol with black wavy hair and burning black eyes, he uses his charms solely to advance himself.

Pavel Syerov   Although he stayed home with a cold during the opening battles of the revolution, Pavel Syerov portrays himself as a true revolutionary. A bit of a dandy who sees himself as a lady's man, Pavel uses Comrade Sonia Presniakova to further his party aims. His plan backfires when she becomes pregnant and blackmails him into marrying her. While spouting the party line, Syerov secretly backs the blackmarket speculations of Karp Morozov and Leo Kovalensky. His party connections save him when his blackmarket dealings are uncovered; his hypocrisy continues when he uses Andrei Taganov's funeral as an opportunity for self-aggrandizement.

Night of January 16th

John Graham Whitfield   Extremely wealthy, impeccably dressed, and distinguished looking, John Whitfield is a man who is used to getting what he wants. President of Whitfield National Bank, he extends a ten million dollar loan to Bjorn Faulkner to buy Faulkner for his daughter. The testimonies of "Guts" Regan and Siegurd Jungquist indicate that when Whitfield realizes that Faulkner had extorted his money and was planning a fake suicide, he killed Faulkner and burned the body.

Nancy Lee Whitfield Faulkner   Young, beautiful, and blonde, Nancy Lee Whitfield Faulkner is, by her testimony, a bereaved widow. Other testimony, however, indicates that she bought Bjorn Faulkner, well aware that he did not care for her, and that she had tried to force him to give up Karen Andre.

Anthem

World Council of Scholars   Supposedly a council of the wisest in all the lands, the World Council of Scholars will not accept the gift of electricity because it was not discovered collectively and also because it may ruin the Department of Candles. They teach that the earth is flat and that the sun revolves around it. Their response to new discovery and invention is to order its destruction and the punishment of the discoverer.

The Fountainhead

Peter Keating   "I am a parasite," Peter Keating tells Howard Roark, and in that statement of self-recognition, he aptly characterizes his villainy and his weakness. Because he wants to feel superior, Keating blackmails, plagiarizes, and beguiles his way to the top of his field. His natural attributes of dark good looks and easy popularity are used to ingratiate himself with his superiors. He moves easily from star of the student body at the Stanton Institute of Technology to rising young architect in the firm of Francon & Heyer by becoming whatever people want him to be. He marries Dominique Francon, whom he does not love, for the prestige, and thereby fails Katie Halsey, the only woman he does love. He then sells Dominique for the Stoneridge commission. By the age of thirty-nine, he is a miserable has-been, and although he understands the nature of his betrayal of self, he is too weak and dependent to change. His presence at Roark's trial has little impact because there is no being left in the shell of his body.

Ellsworth Monkton Toohey   Rand's most self-aware villain, Toohey knows how to control people and chooses the role of soul-collector over other courses in life. His method is to find weaknesses and prey on them. An aunt who sees through him says, "You're a maggot, Elsie. . . . You feed on sores." "Then I'll never starve" is his reply. By making humans feel small, guilty, and low, he helps kill their integrity. Preaching selflessness and egolessness and destroying people's hierarchy of values does all this. Toohey's desire is to be the great leveler, to extinguish all desire to excel. Fragile-looking, like a "chicken just emerging from the egg," he uses a sonorous, velvetlike voice to manipulate people. Although he is often quite direct and tells many that he is dangerous, no one takes him seriously—they assume he is joking. Toohey succeeds in winning his case to make Gail Wynand rehire him on the *Banner*, but

Wynand stops the presses on the day of Toohey's return. Toohey then goes to work for the *Courier*, a prestigious paper, and continues his manipulative ways.

Atlas Shrugged

Dr. Floyd Ferris   His dark good looks, six-foot frame, and mustache make Dr. Floyd Ferris a Valentino type, but his actions are more like the Grand Inquisitor. He invents the Ferris Persuader to torture without killing. His is a theory of control by guilt and when that does not work, blackmail is his fallback technique. He uses the resources of the Science Institute to deride reason and logic in his book *Why Do You Think You Think?* He uses Dr. Robert Stadler, at first with feigned respect, but then with contempt when he knows he is in control.

Wesley Mouch   Wesley Mouch begins as Hank Rearden's man in Washington, but he quickly betrays Rearden to become the assistant coordinator for the Bureau of Economic Planning and National Resources. James Taggart engineers the double cross. Squarish and pale looking with a petulant lower lip and egglike eyes, Mouch never smiles. He rises quickly in Washington, advanced by mediocrity-loving people. When his programs do not work, he whines for greater powers. He pushes Directive 10–289 to achieve stasis and becomes the economic director of the country.

Lillian Rearden   Hank Rearden's wife, Lillian Rearden, is thought of as a glacial and classical beauty, full of gaiety and liveliness. It is all outward show; her eyes are lifeless. She wants her husband to make her happy, but she does not know what it will take. She does not appreciate Hank's worth, condescendingly grants him his marital rights as if they were shameful, and displays his gift of a bracelet of Rearden metal against diamonds to make it look tacky. She delivers her husband over to his enemies and delights in being instrumental in taking Rearden Metal away from him.

Dr. Robert Stadler   Once recognized as the greatest physicist of his time, Dr. Robert Stadler sacrifices his integrity to be freed from material concerns. As the young head of the physics department at Patrick Henry University, he teaches Francisco d'Anconia, Ragnar Danneskjöld, and John Galt, but he loses their respect despite his abilities. He allows himself to be used by Dr. Ferris, rationalizing all the while. When he has the opportunity to denounce the State Science Institute, he is too cowardly to do so. Because of his genius, he is the guiltiest of the villains.

James Taggart   Dagny's brother and president of Taggart Transcontinental, James Taggart looks near fifty although he is only thirty-nine. Wan, petulant, and irritable, his greatest fear is that he will be held responsible for anything. He is a parasite of the first order, always relying on Dagny to get him out of trouble and attempting to ride Francisco d'Anconia's coattails to riches. He marries Cherryl Brooks because he thinks she is beneath him and will therefore adore him. He and Lillian Rearden connive to keep Hank Rearden in line. In his desire to kill John Galt, he finally comes face to face with his hatred of existence.

SECONDARY UNWORTHY OR VILLAINOUS CHARACTERS

Whether they are aiding and abetting the villains in their rise to power or personifying and perpetuating the evils of collectivism, altruism, or mysticism, Rand's secondary unworthy and villainous characters swarm over her literary canvas like Hogarth's inhabitants of Gin Lane or Breughel's villagers. Rand's satire of and invective against a large part of society is often capsulized in her miniportraits of secondary characters. The number and variety of these lesser beings increases as her message became clearer and more encompassing. By the time she wrote *Atlas Shrugged*, the list included representatives from such far-flung areas as train engineering, composing, and sociology.

We the Living

Galina Petrova Argounova   The mother of Kira Argounova, Galina Petrova Argounova is a completely adaptable person. Although she denounces communism privately, she spouts the party line in front of party members. She throws Kira out when she finds Kira has been sleeping with Leo Kovalensky, but later calls marriage a bourgeois prejudice. Eventually, she becomes totally enculturated and teaches in a Labor school.

Lydia Argounova   Kira's older sister, Lydia Argounova is a talented pianist who takes comfort in spirituality. She is conventional, small-spirited, and generally unhappy, but she does not understand why.

Comrade Bitiuk   The office manager at the House of the Peasant and Kira's boss, Comrade Bitiuk is a tall, thin, stern woman who is in total sympathy with the Communist regime.

Rita Eksler   Audacious and sexually aggressive, Rita Eksler is a woman who goes through three husbands.

Vava Nilovskaia   The daughter of a gynecologist who prospers under the new Soviet regime, Vava Nilovskaia tries to retain some of the gaiety of earlier times. She is in love with Victor Dunaev, but when she finds him with Marisha Lavrova, she first makes love to Leo Kovalensky and then marries Kolya Smiatkin on the rebound.

Karp (Koko) Karpovitch Morozov   A large, blond, heavyset man who engages in illegal speculation, Karp (Koko) Karpovitch Morozov keeps Tonia Platoshkina as a mistress and uses Leo Kovalensky as a front man for his speculative business ventures because Leo is the perfect fall guy.

Antonina (Tonia) Pavlovna Platoshkina   A large, garish woman who meets Leo at the sanatorium, Antonia (Tonia) Pavlovna Platoshkina is Koko Morozov's mistress and later keeps Leo as a gigolo.

Comrade Sonia Presniakova   Ambitious and aggressive, Comrade Sonia Presniakova has her mind set on marrying Pavel Syerov. She accomplishes this by becoming pregnant and then exerting subtle political blackmail. She has political savvy and uses it to attain party power.

Kolya Smiatkin   Hopelessly and doggedly devoted to Vava Nilovskaia, Kolya Smiatkin is young, blond, and chubby. He acts as vice-secretary of the club library without pay in order to avoid losing his job.

Night of January 16th

District Attorney Flint   In his closing argument, District Attorney Flint, Karen Andre's prosecutor, calls for the jury to uphold common standards and crush the concept of man as conqueror.

Magda Swanson   The Faulkner family housekeeper for thirty-eight years, Magda Swanson is plain, religious, middle-aged, and hates Karen Andre. She thinks Karen is a sinful and shameless woman and testifies against her at the trial.

The Fountainhead

Mr. and Mrs. Dale Ainsworth   Mr. and Mrs. Dale Ainsworth own the gray granite, late Renaissance home, which Peter Keating designed; Dominique Francon ridicules it in her column.

Allen   Allen the slotman, head of the copy desk at the *Banner*, is fired by Gail Wynand for disobeying orders.

Athelstan Beasley   The head of the Arts Ball and general wit of the world of architecture, Athelstan Beasley writes a column and organizes social events; he does little designing and building, however.

Caleb Bradley   A crooked entrepreneur, who sells 200 percent of the Monadnock Valley summer resort project, Caleb Bradley chooses Howard Roark as its architect because he thinks that Roark will ensure its failure.

Sally Brent   The *Banner* resident sob sister, Sally Brent breaks Gail Wynand's ban on writing about Mrs. Gail Wynand; Brent writes a treacly account of the marriage, which gets her fired. She then writes an exposé of Wynand's love life for the *New Frontiers*.

Dwight Carson   Although he begins as a writer of great integrity, Dwight Carson is bought by Gail Wynand and forced to write for the masses. He becomes a dipsomaniac.

Lancelot Clokey   A foreign correspondent who has written a bestseller about his personal adventures in foreign countries, Lancelot Clokey uses significant world events as a backdrop for recounting his sordid experiences; only Ellsworth Toohey's advocacy makes the book sell.

Lois Cook   The author of *The Gallant Gallstone*, Lois Cook is a thirty-seven-year-old woman who likes to say she is sixty-four. She has no delusions about the quality of her work but argues that worth is not important and that words should be freed from the stranglehold of reason. A large, unkempt woman who lives on inherited money, she wants to build the ugliest house in New York because anyone can build a nice-looking house. She is part of Toohey's inner circle.

Tim Davis   Peter Keating's first step on his rise in Francon & Heyer is to supplant Tim Davis as favored draftsman. Tim allows Peter to do much of his work; Tim's energies are devoted to his romance and subsequent marriage. He is frequently late for work and soon gets fired.

Dean of the Stanton Institute of Technology   Although he perfunctorily tries to soften Howard Roark's expulsion from Stanton, the Dean of the Stanton Institute of Technology realizes that his advice has no impact on Roark. Horrified at Roark's attitude, the Dean calls Roark a dangerous man.

Neil Dumont   A poor designer, but a man with aristocratic connections, Neil Dumont becomes Peter Keating's best friend. When Guy Francon retires, Dumont becomes Keating's partner.

Mrs. Dunlop   A young and attractive woman, Mrs. Dunlop is persuaded by Peter Keating to hire Claude Stengel as the architect for her home. This commission gives Stengel the start he needs to leave Francon & Heyer, thereby moving Keating up to the position of chief designer.

Falk   A copyreader for the *Banner*, Falk is fired along with Allen, Mr. Harding, and Ellsworth Toohey.

Jules Fougler   The drama critic for the *Banner* and one of Toohey's inner circle, Jules Fougler is a saggy and cynical man who believes that the dramatist is irrelevant and the daily life of the common man can just as readily be critiqued for its artistic points. He decides to make Ike's wretched play, *No Skin off Your Ass*, a hit, just because it is such a poor play.

Mrs. Gillespie   Tall, toothy, dripping in diamonds, Mrs. Gillespie cannot believe that Ellsworth Toohey can be a radical because he is not dirty.

Mr. Harding   The sixty-year-old managing editor of the *Banner*, Mr. Harding is fired by Gail Wynand for allowing Toohey's anti-Roark article to be printed. Harding's wife writes a response published under his name in *New Frontiers*.

Lucius N. Heyer   A collector of old porcelain who looks like he has just been bled, Lucius N. Heyer is the last of a dissipated old bloodline. He is Guy Francon's partner, chosen for his monied connections. He is generally ineffectual in the firm and leaves his share to Peter Keating.

Constance (Kiki) Holcombe   A small, perky, and vivacious woman who tries to look younger than her forty-two years, Constance (Kiki) Holcombe collects famous people in her architects' salon. She has made a career of entertaining.

Ralston Holcombe   The president of the Architect's Guild of America, Ralston Holcombe is a round, pink man with a mane of white hair who dresses outlandishly and affects a temperament of artistic bravura. His specialty is state buildings and monuments, and he is obsessed with Renaissance style.

Ike   The author of *No Skin off Your Ass*, which is produced under the title *No Skin off Your Nose*, Ike is a talentless twenty-six-year-old playwright who has written eleven unproduced plays. He does not see why talent ought to be a factor in writing plays.

Mr. Nathaniel Janss   Bullied by Austen Heller into giving Howard Roark a chance at a commission for the Janss-Stuart Real Estate Company office building, Nathaniel Janss agrees with Roark's arguments for not building with unnecessary ornamentation. However, he cannot hold out against his board of directors.

Mrs. Louisa Keating   Mrs. Louisa Keating is Peter's mother and is the prototype of the self-sacrificing and directive mother who influences her son away from art and into architecture, away from the woman he loves and toward a woman with more social prominence. She does not understand why Peter ends up such a miserable man.

Vincent Knowlton   One of Peter Keating's crowd, Vincent Knowlton is characterized as innocuous by Dominique Francon.

Eve Layton   A beautiful woman whose main desire is to be avant-garde, Eve Layton is very athletic. Her careless intellectual leaps parallel her athletic leaps. Her husband, Mitchell Layton, hates her.

Mitchell Layton   A pouting, obnoxious young man who feels guilty about his inheritance, Mitchell Layton slouches about mouthing ideas that espouse more societal regulation and less choice. He buys part of the *Banner* and helps Toohey undermine Wynand.

Robert Mundy   Sent by Austen Heller to Howard Roark, Robert Mundy is obsessed with recreating for himself a symbol of his rise from poverty. He wants Roark to copy the premier mansion in the county in which he grew up. Roark cannot convince him to build a monument to his own rather than someone else's success.

Eugene Pettingill   In his seventies and most unattractive, Eugene Pettingill is one of the conventional architects who speaks out against Roark's work.

Jessica Pratt   A woman whose guiding principle is unselfishness, Jessica Pratt has dedicated her life to her sister, Renee Slottern.

Gordon J. Prescott   A tall, tanned, blond, athletic-looking man with the demeanor of a university man, Gordon J. Prescott always wears turtlenecks. He keeps Roark waiting two-and-a-half hours for their first appointment. Although he writes an article about his encouragement of talented newcomers, Prescott's idea of originality is reproduction of old forms into new purposes. He calls his approach utilitarian and pragmatic.

June Sanborn   The nineteen-year-old daughter of Whitford Sanborn, June Sanborn has romantic preconceptions about architects, and when Howard Roark does not respond to her flirtation, she proclaims her hatred for the house he designs.

Whitford Sanborn   Because he has been so satisfied with an office building that Henry Cameron designed for him, Whitford Sanborn takes Cameron's advice and contracts with Roark to build a country home. Although he loves the modern home that Roark builds for him, he is too weak to hold out against his wife's refusal to live in it.

Mrs. Whitford Sanborn   A woman who cares more about what her friends think of her home and appearance than anything else, Mrs. Whitford Sanborn tries to sabotage Roark's plans for her new country house at every turn. When the house is built, she refuses to live in it.

Alvah Scarret   Although he looks like a kindly country doctor, and although he had been totally devoted to Gail Wynand and the *Banner*, Alvah Scarret aids Ellsworth Toohey in his takeover plans. Scarret is editor-in-chief and Dominique Francon's boss when she works at the *Banner*. Vehemently opposed to Wynand's marriage to Dominique, he tries to convince Wynand that he should not marry her. When Dominique goes to Roark, Scarret is the one who takes the news to Wynand and insists on a divorce. He then uses the paper to create the image of

Wynand as the victim of a depraved woman with whom he was madly infatuated.

Homer Slottern   A man who is ashamed of his ownership of three department stores, Homer Slottern feels that he has neglected his spiritual growth. He dresses ostentatiously, believes theories are nonsense, and joins the group that buys part of the *Banner* in order to undermine Wynand.

Renee Slottern   Renee Slottern, Homer's wife, is a vacant and naive woman. Jessica Pratt, her sister, has dedicated her life to Renee's upbringing.

John Erik Snyte   The head of an architecture firm that includes one architect for each style, John Erick Snyte hires Howard Roark to be the modernist. After each architect submits a plan, Snyte makes an amalgam of their work. Snyte bastardizes Roark's plans for Austen Heller's house and then fires Roark when he corrects the plans in Heller's presence. He tries to rehire Roark when he finds out that Heller has given him the commission.

Hopton Stoddard   A smiling little man who has taken refuge in religion as he has grown older, Hopton Stoddard plans a nondenominational temple to leave as a monument to faith. He is totally under the influence of Ellsworth Toohey and files suit against Roark for breach of contract and malpractice when the temple does not reflect his vision of faith.

Joel Sutton   A badminton-playing, "smiling ball of meat," Joel Sutton lacks any discrimination—he loves everything and everyone. At first he chooses Roark as his architect because Roger Enright has, but then he takes the commission away because Dominique Francon suggests that Peter Keating would be a more popular choice.

Mrs. Mary Toohey   Ellsworth Toohey's mother loves him from the moment he is born because he is so uninspiring of love. Mrs. Mary Toohey is an erratic woman who goes through a number of religions but idolizes only Ellsworth. She constantly nags his father to get things for Ellsworth.

Gus Webb   A crude-talking, tough, socially ungracious architect who leads the "We Don't Read Wynand" movement, Gus Webb is the vicious kind of individual who is sorry there were no people in the Cortlandt project when Roark blew it up.

Atlas Shrugged

Mayor Bascom   Mayor Bascom is the dingily dressed, pear-shaped, and unprincipled mayor of the dying town of Rome, Wisconsin. He tells Dagny Taggart part of the story of Twentieth Century Motors.

Luke Beal   The fireman of the doomed Comet, Luke Beal is one who thought his superiors knew what they were doing.

Dr. Blodgett   A young, fattish scientist, Dr. Blodgett is the man who pulls the lever to demonstrate Project X.

Orren Boyle   A large, loud man with slitlike eyes, Orren Boyle is the head of Associated Steel. He makes a fortune with government money. Because his business is not successful, he wants to limit Hank Rearden and make the most of government subsidies. He also pushes to open patents so that he can produce Rearden Metal. When Rearden quits, Boyle has a nervous breakdown.

Laura Bradford   A movie actress who made her way to the top by sleeping with bureaucrats, Laura Bradford is Kip Chalmers's mistress.

Kip Chalmers   A second rater from the semipowerful ranks of bureaucrats, Kip Chalmers is running for the legislature of California.

Emma "Ma" Chalmers   After her son's death in the Taggart Tunnel disaster, Emma "Ma" Chalmers becomes something of a celebrity. A mystic and a Buddhist, Ma tries to convert the country to a soybean diet, a disastrous scheme that ruins the wheat harvest.

Balph Eubank   The literary leader of the period, Balph Eubank believes that "plot is a primitive vulgarity in literature." Eubank also feels that the essence of life is defeat and suffering; therefore, that is what literature should reveal.

Señor Rodrigo Gonzalez   A man who looks like a killer, Señor Rodrigo Gonzalez is famous for his parties. He is the diplomatic representative of Chile who joined the regime that nationalized his property.

Señora Gonzalez   An asset to her husband because she helps influence people in his favor, Señora Gonzalez has the reputation of being a beauty due to the frenetic quality of energy she displays.

Tinky Holloway   A rat-faced, slim, slouching man who is described in tennis imagery, Tinky Holloway is one of the influence peddlers along with James Taggart, Wesley Mouch, Chick Morrison, Cuffy Meigs, Dr. Ferris, and Mr. Thompson. He explains the Steel Unification plan to Hank Rearden.

Lee Hunsacker   A worn-out has-been at forty-two, Lee Hunsacker blames everyone but himself for his failures. He heads the Amalgamated Service, which takes over Twentieth Century Motors, and brings suit against Midas Mulligan for not loaning him money. His suit precipitates the withdrawal of Mulligan and Judge Narragansett from a looter's society.

Fred Kinnan   A racketeer who heads Amalgamated Labor of America, Fred Kinnan is one of the most honest of the looters. He does not pretend that he is doing anything else. He calls the actions of the government an "anti-industrial revolution" and points out the pitfalls of its actions or lack of action.

Gilbert Keith-Worthing   A seventy-year-old British novelist, Gilbert Keith-Worthing is an author whose world fame consists of books that have not been read. His line is that since there is no such thing as freedom, people should not mind the tyranny of a dictatorship. Flabby, obese, and cynical, he is Kip Chalmers's guest on the Comet.

Paul Larkin   An unsuccessful man who takes advantage of his friendship with the Rearden family, Paul Larkin takes over the Rearden ore mines under the Equalization Bill. Although he assures Hank Rearden that his ownership is only a technicality and that he will continue providing ore, he does not. Short, plump, and boyish at fifty-three, he is one who wheedles and whines and rationalizes his failures.

Eugene Lawson   When the Community Bank of Madison that he heads goes bankrupt, Eugene Lawson gets a job in Washington, D.C., with the Bureau of Economic Planning and National Resources. He preaches the line that personal goals do not matter and that it is everyone's social obligation to produce. He calls the mind corrupt and declares that it is the Age of Love rather than Reason.

Mort Liddy   A composer of old-fashioned movie scores, Mort Liddy also popularizes and mangles Richard Halley's concerto to win an award as best movie score of the year.

Clifton Locey   A master at not taking responsibility for any action, Clifton Locey is a friend of Jim Taggart who takes the position of vice-president of operation when Dagny Taggart quits. He knows little about and cares nothing for the railroad; his only goal is to please Taggart and Washington, D.C.

Cuffy Meigs   An ignorant, uncouth lout, of bulging girth and nasal voice, Cuffy Meigs is the director of unification. He takes over Project X and drunkenly and stupidly pulls the wrong lever on the xylophone.

David Mitchum   Because the good men have quit and because he has pull, David Mitchum becomes the superintendent of the Colorado Division of Taggart Transcontinental, but he shirks his decision-making responsibilities.

Chick Morrison   A nonentity who serves as Morale Conditioner, Chick Morrison resigns after John Galt's speech.

Horace Bussby Mowen   Although he is president of Amalgamated Switch and Signal Company of Connecticut, Horace Bussby Mowen will not make switches of Rearden Metal because the people do not like the brand. When public opinion changes, so does his. He believes in the

Equalization of Opportunity Bill and is the show industrialist for the government.

Ben Nealy   Soft, bulky, and sullen, Ben Nealy is a contractor who replaces Dick McNamara. He complains about Ellis Wyatt, though Wyatt takes care of problems that should be attended to by Nealy.

Betty Pope   A member of one of the best families, Betty Pope is a homely woman who sleeps with Jim Taggart.

Dr. Potter   As a representative from the State Science Institute, Dr. Potter attempts to discourage Hank Rearden's marketing of Rearden Metal. When he fails, he attempts to buy it.

Dr. Simon Pritchett   The author of *The Metaphysical Contradictions of the Universe*, Dr. Simon Pritchett preaches the doctrine that human beings are just chemistry and biology and everything is a matter of opinion. His premise is that "logic is a primitive vulgarity of philosophy."

Mrs. Rearden   Hank Rearden's mother is a nagging, critical, reproachful woman who only knows how to take. Mrs. Rearden does not appreciate her son's abilities and seeks to keep him bound by guilt. Her definition of virtue is giving to the undeserving.

Philip Rearden   Rather than appreciating his brother Hank's charity, Philip Rearden lives in Hank's home and criticizes him. A sickly, tired man, he works for organizations and then spies on his brother for the government.

Joe Scott   Although he has broken the safety rules and has been fired from other jobs, Joe Scott becomes the engineer for Taggart Transcontinental because of his friendship with Fred Kinnan. He goes to work drunk and is the engineer for the Comet disaster.

Bertram Scudder   The editor of *The Future* magazine, Bertram Scudder writes nasty articles about Hank Rearden. He is the broadcaster on the radio program that Dagny Taggart uses to denounce the government for its blackmailing of Hank Rearden. His tone is an attempt to sound "cynical, skeptical, superior, and hysterical together."

Claude Slagenhop   The president of Friends for Global Progress, Claude Slagenhop believes that need is the only consideration. A collectivist through and through, he thinks that there is no source for public opinion, only the collective instinct of the collective mind.

Gerald Starnes   Once the heir to Twentieth Century Motors, Gerald Starnes is found in a flophouse, willing to sell his name for a drink. With his sister, Ivy, he had attempted to institute a collectivist system at the factory.

Ivy Starnes   When she and her brothers inherit Twentieth Century Motors, Ivy Starnes institutes a plan to run it by the precept "From each according to his ability, to each according to his need." When the plan ruins the plant, she retires to Eastern religions and a foul-smelling Mississippi bungalow.

Mr. Thompson   A nondescript, wilted looking man, Mr. Thompson schemes his way to becoming head of state. He is a product of chance who is willing to be flexible about everything and whose code of belief is that everyone is open to a deal.

Lester Tuck   Kip Chalmers's press agent, Lester Tuck is an ex-attorney who used to represent shoplifters.

Clem Weatherby   Washington's man on the Taggart Transcontinental board, Clem Weatherby is an influence trader. He is the one who suggests that James Taggart keep Rearden in line.

NEUTRAL OR METAMORPHOSING CHARACTERS

There are few characters who are presented neutrally in Rand's works because, by her moral premises, humans all have choices and therefore are responsible for their actions or inaction. Most of the neutral characters in her early works are functionaries for plot purposes; by the time Rand wrote *Atlas Shrugged*, she had classified almost every character in either a positive or a negative class. Besides the neutral individuals, this section also includes the metamorphosing characters—those who begin in one group and then through re-evaluation or experience move to the opposite camp. They are few but still possible in Rand's perception of character.

Classifying Eddie Willers, however, does present a problem. He is neither neutral nor metamorphosing. Although there is reason to believe that Rand meant him to be a positive character, he never does learn the lessons the other heroes learn. He is left stranded on a frozen train, perhaps a metaphor for his indeterminate status.

We the Living

Alexander Dimitrievitch Argounov   Once the owner of a granite mansion and a textile factory, Alexander Dimitrievitch Argounov is the father of the Argounov family and is reduced by Soviet nationalization to a bookkeeping job. He is a caring but ineffectual man.

Acia Dunaev   Sister to Victor and Irina Dunaev, Acia Dunaev is young and bratty.

Maria (Marussia) Petrovna Dunaev   Sallow and sickly looking, the mother of the Dunaev family, Maria (Marussia) Petrovna Dunaev, was once a great beauty but due to poor medical care dies hemorrhaging and coughing.

Marina Marisha Lavrova   Marina Marisha Lavrova begins as a not-too-bright, slovenly member of Komsomol, the Communist Union of Youth, and is convinced by Victor Dunaev to take over one of the rooms belonging to Leo Kovalensky and Kira Argounova. However, when Marisha later marries Victor, she is kind to her father-in-law and sneaks help to Irina Dunaev and Sasha Chernov against Victor's wishes.

Night of January 16th

James Chandler   New York Police Department's handwriting expert, James Chandler is a precise and dignified man who testifies that Bjorn Faulkner's suicide note is not forged.

Court Bailiff and Court Clerk   The Court Bailiff and Court Clerk perform their appropriate functions in court. Unremarkable, they serve as perfunctory characters.

Judge Heath   The judge of the case of *The People of the State of New York v. Karen Andre*, Judge Heath presides in a straightforward and impartial manner.

John Hutchins   The shy, nervous watchman of the Faulkner Building, John Hutchins testifies to letting Karen Andre, Bjorn Faulkner, and two other men into the building on the night of January 16th.

Dr. Kirkland   The elderly and kindly medical examiner, Dr. Kirkland testifies to the condition of the body presumed to be Bjorn Faulkner.

Elmer Sweeney   Elmer Sweeney is the police inspector who investigates the possible murder/suicide of Bjorn Faulkner and is awed by the perfumed water in the bathroom of Karen's penthouse.

Homer Van Fleet   A private investigator hired by Nancy Lee Faulkner to follow Bjorn Faulkner, Homer Van Fleet testifies to what he saw on the night of January 16th: he saw Karen Andre push a body over the parapet of her penthouse.

The Fountainhead

Miss Cameron   Miss Cameron, Henry Cameron's sister, is a meek, elderly, emotionless woman who assumes his care when Cameron collapses.

Guy Francon   Although he is first pictured as a middle-aged, self-satisfied architect who made his name by designing the Frink National Bank Building, a miasma of columns, frills, and furbelows, Guy Francon begins to question his values. At first he represents what Peter Keating strives to be, but then he rejects the actions of his fellow architects during the Stoddard trial. Initially he is made uncomfortable by his daughter Dominique, but during her divorce from Gail Wynand, Francon invites her to stay with him and provides support and approval.

Catherine (Katie) Halsey   In 1921 when she comes to live with her uncle Ellsworth Toohey, Catherine (Katie) Halsey is young and uncomplicated, flush with the expectation of a glowing future. Plain and a bit clumsy, she nevertheless makes Peter Keating feel wonderful as they fall in love and plan marriage. With the destruction of her dreams, she becomes first a bitter and then a petty, take-charge person who is indifferent to Peter and has obliterated thoughts of the past. Katie is one of the few Rand characters who moves from positive to negative.

Richard Sanborn   Although he is considered a drunken wastrel, Whitford Sanborn's son Richard has enough judgment to appreciate the house Howard Roark builds and to insist on living there.

Ted Shlinker   Peter Keating's competition for outstanding student at Stanton Institute of Technology, Ted Shlinker is outdistanced by Peter in the final year.

Claude Stengel   A small, bony, angular man who cannot be bought by friendship, Claude Stengel, who does all of Guy Francon's designing, is Peter Keating's second step on the ladder up the Francon & Heyer hierarchy. Stengel correctly assesses Keating's perfidy.

Mr. Weidler   A friend of Richard Sanborn, Mr. Weidler is on the board of Metropolitan Bank Company and gets the bank board to accept Roark's drawing, although he gives in to the condition of a classical facade.

Atlas Shrugged

Cherryl Brooks Taggart   When she meets James Taggart, who she thinks is the unsung hero of Taggart Transcontinental, Cherryl Brooks is nineteen, starry-eyed, and works in a dime store. She is so enthralled with Jim's attention that she drowns her doubts. Initially hostile to Dagny, she learns slowly and painfully that Dagny is what she thought Jim was. She apologizes to Dagny but does not have the strength to cope with the horrors she encounters and thus runs through the darkness over a parapet to her death.

Wet Nurse (Tony)   Put into Rearden Mills by Washington to act as an enforcer of government policies, Tony, or Wet Nurse, the name given him by the steel workers, starts as a cynic who does not believe in absolutes. He comes to admire Hank Rearden, tells Rearden to do as he pleases and that he will juggle the books so Washington will not know. He eventually gives his life to protect Rearden's mills.

Eddie Willers   The special assistant to the vice-president of operations of Taggart Transcontinental, Eddie Willers is a retainer of the Taggart family as his forefathers were before him. Fair, direct, and fiercely loyal to Dagny and Taggart Transcontinental, Eddie is culpable in two areas: He discloses Dagny's private business to an unknown railroad worker who turns out to be John Galt; he cannot quit and continues to let the leeches use his abilities.

CHAPTER 4

The Nonfiction

Ayn Rand's fiction brought her to the attention of many young intellectuals for whom she filled a need that had been starved by the prevailing existential, relativistic, and Marxist philosophies. With *Atlas Shrugged*, she enhanced and completed what she had accomplished on a lesser scale in *The Fountainhead*: John Galt is her portrayal of an ideal man who is all that Howard Roark was and more; not only does she provide the portrait of one ideal man, but she embellishes it with her depiction of three others on a similar scale; to complete her ideal cast of characters, she creates the ideal woman, Dagny Taggart. Rand had achieved the goal she set for herself as a writer. Furthermore, she created for these ideal characters the opportunity to fulfill the ultimate fantasy: righting all the world's wrongs. After *Atlas Shrugged*, Rand published no more fiction. It is easy to understand why. She had fulfilled her destiny as an imaginative writer; she had created an ideal world peopled with ideal characters. *Atlas Shrugged*, like the Bible, remains the main myth (I define *myth* as the narrative that embodies the dogma and values of a particular group) to which her subsequent philosophical essays continually refer.

The second stage of Rand's career as a writer developed naturally as a result of the interest her works of fiction aroused in readers for whom the thought content was as, if not more, important than the plot and characters. Of course, there are many readers whose appetites are quite satisfied by the exciting stories and whose interest does not go beyond the fiction.

In the interim between the publication of *The Fountainhead* and *Atlas Shrugged*, Rand had established a close relationship with Nathaniel and Barbara Branden. That association had a significant effect on the direction of her writing career. Her informal meetings with them to discuss the larger implications of her philosophy led, after the publication of

Atlas Shrugged, to the formation of classes by which more students could be introduced to her philosophy, Objectivism. Under the auspices of the Nathaniel Branden Lectures, the first course, "The Basic Principles of Objectivism," was taught by Nathaniel Branden. It developed into the Nathaniel Branden Institute (NBI), which offered courses as diverse as the application of Objectivism to psychology, economics, and esthetics. Ayn Rand's ideas are marketable in and of themselves and marketing them is what her nonfiction books do.

Rand published six books of nonfiction in her lifetime: *For the New Intellectual* (1961); *The Virtue of Selfishness* (1964); *Capitalism: The Unknown Ideal* (1966); *The Romantic Manifesto* (1969); *The New Left: The Anti-Industrial Revolution* (1971); *Introduction to Objectivist Epistemology* (1979). The book *Philosophy: Who Needs It* (1982) was in process but was not published until after her death. *The Voice of Reason: Essays in Objectivist Thought* was not published until 1988. All of Rand's nonfiction books are largely compilations of materials that were published previously, either in fiction or in the various Objectivist publications. None are composed of predominately original text. Some of the pieces are reproductions of speeches that Rand delivered in such diverse fora as West Point graduation exercises or the Ford Hall Forum. Publishing these assorted pieces in book form makes them more accessible to the general public.

Another category of Rand's nonfiction is the posthumously published materials. These include everything from notes for a daily schedule in her latter years to harsh evaluations of other writers penned in the margins of her books. Brief summaries of the edited versions of her letters, journals, and marginalia follow the summaries of the compilations of her essays.

The main sources for her nonfiction books were her periodicals, newsletters, or journals. These publications provided a far-reaching and effective method of disseminating not only the tenets of Objectivist philosophy, but also information about activities of interest to the growing number of adherents to and students of Rand's ideas. Through the newsletters, both Rand and Branden could reach a larger audience than they could in the classroom setting. On January 1, 1962, with Barbara Branden as managing editor, they undertook the publication of *The Objectivist Newsletter*, which was dedicated to explaining the application of Objectivism to contemporary problems. A fuller discussion of these newsletters follows in the summary section of this chapter. Increased circulation caused the *Newsletter* to be enlarged and presented in a magazine format, which was called simply *The Objectivist*. It began publication in January 1966. In 1971, the monthly magazine was replaced by a less formal newsletter, which Rand described as "a personal communication." *The Ayn Rand Letter* was issued fortnightly in response to the need for a wider arena. It is in these various periodicals that Rand first published the essays and treatises that were later anthologized and collected into suitable groupings for the books.

From 1980 to 1987, *The Objectivist Forum*, a bimonthly journal, continued the dissemination of Objectivist ideas. Founded with the cooperation of Rand, and edited initially by Harry Binswanger, it included twelve of her essays.

What follows are summary discussions of Rand's major nonfiction publications. Each book is discussed individually, but the periodicals are discussed in three groups according to title. Summarizing anthologies is difficult. One must either summarize each of the component essays or opt for generalizations about the overall impact of the book. I have chosen the latter. In some cases, I mention certain specific essays for their ability to communicate the sense of the anthology. Different readers may find different emphases more to their liking. Rand's nonfiction works address complex and difficult issues, and her methodology is to dig for the roots of the problem and then ascend point by point to her conclusion. Therefore, it is imperative, if the reader is to understand the reasoning behind Rand's philosophical premises, that he or she read the original essays. The purpose of these summaries is to give those who have not read the works some idea of what may be found in them. The works are arranged chronologically, in order of publication dates.

FOR THE NEW INTELLECTUAL (1961)

Subtitled "The Philosophy of Ayn Rand," this book was originally published by Random House, first in hardcover and then in paperback. For those who are interested in a capsulized version of the major themes of her fiction, this is a good place to start. The book is a compilation of excerpts from her four novels. Each excerpt is prefaced by a note in which Rand explains the context of the particular speech. As her novels became progressively more overtly didactic as well as lengthy, there are many more pages of speeches from *Atlas Shrugged* than from the other three novels combined. Eight major speeches from that novel are included; three from *The Fountainhead*; one each from *We the Living* and *Anthem*. It is in this book that Rand first publicly names her philosophy Objectivism.

The major attraction for those who have already read the novels, besides the pleasure of having all the major themes supplied in one volume, is the introductory essay in which Rand explains the background that underlies the necessity for a new group of intellectuals. Her major premises are that the historical culprits—spiritual in the forms of the church or other institutions of faith and physical in the forms of chiefs, kings, or governments—have combined to undermine the progress of individuals toward personal happiness. She calls these two forces The

Witch Doctor and Attila. A third force is personified in The Producer or the reasoning person, the thinker. It is the third that is representative of the best in humanity; Producers, thinkers, reasoners are people who utilize those attributes that make human survival possible.

In Rand's reading of the history of Western civilization, there are two golden periods. The first was during Aristotle's introduction of a philosophy that identified an objective reality. She credits Aristotle with liberating reason, and it was the rediscovery of his works that initiated the Renaissance, according to Rand. The second golden age was introduced by America's Founding Fathers who established in the United States the first society in history that was created by and dominated by men of the mind, thinkers who were men of both word and deed. They inaugurated the economically free nineteenth century, which Rand describes as being the period closest to laissez-faire capitalism that the world has ever achieved. In a capitalistic society, the key figures are the intellectual and the businessman. Rand sees businessmen as great liberators who, through their efforts, freed the masses from eighteen-hour work days and raised the standard of living by making the latest scientific and technological discoveries popularly available. The cause of many of our current problems is that businessmen have accepted unearned guilt promulgated by intellectual altruists.

Rand indicts philosophers who have veered from Aristotelian epistemology; she begins with Descartes and progresses chronologically through Hume, Kant (the archvillain), Hegel, Comte, Marx, and Nietzsche. According to Rand, philosophy has brought us to this miserable state of confusion and ambiguity, and therefore, it is the job of philosophy to lead us out. Each person's philosophy, either explicitly or implicitly, undergirds his or her actions. All who would be intellectuals need to understand their philosophical premises and the implications of those premises.

THE VIRTUE OF SELFISHNESS (1964)

Rand's clarification of the essential definition of selfishness introduces this series of essays, fourteen by Rand and five by Nathaniel Branden. All, except the first, were originally published in The Objectivist Newsletter. "The Objectivist Ethics" is the reproduction of a speech delivered to a University of Wisconsin symposium. The various essays are particularly helpful to a student of Objectivism or interested reader because they clarify basic standards and values of Objectivism from a variety of perspectives.

The introductory essay outlines the rationale of Rand's ethics. She explains that life is the standard by which good is judged; therefore, one's own life should be one's ethical purpose. Values are then chosen to achieve that purpose. Rand identifies Reason, Purpose, and Self-Esteem as the cardinal values of Objectivist ethics; in order to achieve those values, one acts on the virtues that correspond to those values, which are Rationality, Productiveness, and Pride. Rationality incorporates such virtues as Independence, Integrity, Honesty, and Justice—all part of not faking reality. For Rand, maintenance of life and the pursuit of happiness are but two parts of the same whole.

The composition of this book is eclectic. The diversity of subject matter Rand deals with is apparent in the range of her essay titles from "Racism" to "Government Financing in a Free Society." A number of the essays are couched as responses to pervading bromides of contemporary society such as: "Who am I to judge?" or "There is no black or white, only gray," or "All life is compromise." Rand rebuts these ideas in "How Does One Lead a Rational Life in an Irrational Society?" "The Cult of Moral Grayness," and "Doesn't Life Require Compromise?" She challenges the morality and the logic of such popular platitudes and explains why the acceptance of them is detrimental to one's moral health.

Nathaniel Branden's essays on the psychological aspects of Objectivism augment Rand's philosophical perspective. Branden discusses "Counterfeit Individualism" and "The Divine Right of Stagnation." In one of his sections, Branden responds to the popular argument that everyone is basically selfish, so there is no need for a philosophy that encourages selfishness. He also explains in "The Psychology of Pleasure" that the people and things that give one pleasure are a sure indication of one's values. In his discussion of romantic love and its sexual celebration, he sets the stage for ideas he was to develop, among other places, in his book *The Psychology of Romantic Love*.

Montaigne, author of the book *Essais* which created the genre of the essay, defined the essay as "an attempt," a brief discussion as opposed to a thesis or dissertation. These essays are just that—compressed discussions, forays into their subjects. As such, they are appealing to interested nonacademic or nonspecialist readers as well as to the more serious student of Objectivism. *The Virtue of Selfishness* has been one of Rand's best-selling nonfiction works.

CAPITALISM: THE UNKNOWN IDEAL (1966)

In this, the third of Rand's nonfiction books, the first section of theoretical and historical essays includes three articles by Alan Greenspan, one by Robert Hessen, and one by Nathaniel Branden. In the section on the current state of the nation, all the articles are by Rand, except "Alienation," which is written by Nathaniel Branden. Rand calls the book "a collection of essays on the *moral* aspects of capitalism." Since a system of ethics must underlie any political system, Rand also reprints in this book two essays, one on rights and one on the nature of government, which were published in *The Virtue of Selfishness*.

Rand sees capitalism as the only moral politico-economic system in history, a system that has been a great boon to humankind. Her contention is that it is being destroyed because its tenets are not being properly identified even by its loudest adherents (she calls the *Encyclopaedia Britannica* article about "Capitalism" a disgrace). Her purpose is to clearly identify the benefits of capitalism while also exposing the nature of its archenemy, altruism.

War, the gold standard, the property status of the airwaves, and student rebellion are among the diverse subjects discussed in the various essays. Rand sees any initiation of force as wrong and, therefore, concludes that the only moral war is a war of self-defense. She contends that capitalism inaugurated the longest period of peace in Western history: that period between the end of the Napoleonic wars in 1815 and World War I in 1914. Since she sees war as essentially looting, and since societies where there is freedom to produce do not need to loot from others, Rand concludes that capitalistic systems do not cause wars. It was the statist governments that caused World Wars I and II. Rand also thinks that the draft is an infringement on individual rights. In her view, the only good army is a volunteer army and that is what results when a country is under attack as the United States was during World War II.

THE ROMANTIC MANIFESTO (1969)

Much of the appeal of Objectivism is its inclusiveness. Given the basic values and attitudes, one can then form opinions about every subject from abortion to literary criticism. Moving from her definition of art as "a selective re-creation of reality according to an artist's metaphysical value-judgments," Rand then proceeds to show the connections between art and a sense of life, to explain the basic principles of literature, to define Romanticism, and to articulate the goals of her writing. Rand identifies herself as a writer of "Romantic realism" and damns the abandonment of rational esthetics as the cause of the contemporary degradation of art.

The Romantic Manifesto is perhaps the most unified and coherent of Rand's nonfiction works. Rand explains the importance of art to human consciousness. Art concretizes abstractions and thereby provides images that integrate an incalculable number of concepts. Rand's philosophy of literature develops from an Aristotelian base. She reads Aristotle as justifing the importance of literature by explaining that history represents things only as they are, whereas poetry (literature) represents them as they *might be* or *ought to be*. As a medium for communicating a moral ideal, art is indispensable. Communicating moral ideals in the persons of her heroes and heroines is exactly what Rand's art does. If she were to write a dedication page for an anthology of all her works, it would read "To the glory of man," Rand explains.

Rand sees nineteenth-century Romanticism as a product of an Aristotelian sense of life, sans the undergirding philosophy, fueled by capitalism and rebellion against the prevailing Classicist establishment. Ironically, it was the Classicists who were seen as the exemplars of reason and the Romantics as advocates of the *primacy of emotions*; Rand calls this definition by nonessentials and explains that it is the *primacy of values* that distinguished the Romantics. By Rand's definition, the greatest purely Romantic novelists are Victor Hugo and Feodor Dostoevsky; the greatest playwrights, Friedrich Schiller and Edmond Rostand. Novels that she cites for their Romantic vision are *Quo Vadis* and *The Scarlet Letter*. Among second ranked Romanticists, she names Walter Scott and Alexander Dumas. O. Henry, for his zestfully childlike and ever-inventive imagination, is her candidate for the greatest popularizer of Romanticism's psychological mission of making life interesting.

Naturalism is the antithesis of Romanticism. Whereas Romanticism proceeds from a moral base and the concept of human beings as capable of free will, Naturalism attempts a nonjudgmental approach and depicts humans as the victims of a deterministic universe. Rand points out the flaws in this deterministic view. Shakespeare is seen as the spiritual father of nineteenth-century Naturalism with Honoré de Balzac and Leo Tolstoy as his heirs. All maintained an abstract level of characterization, presenting their views on a metaphysical level. Rand admires them more than those who succumbed to Emile Zola's journalistic methods. The title of "the most evil book in serious literature," however, is reserved for *Anna Karenina*, which Rand says carries an antihappiness message. Although she does not agree with their literary philosophy, she cites Sinclair Lewis and John O'Hara as the best representatives of contemporary Naturalism.

A special bonus at the end of the book is Rand's short story "The Simplest Thing in the World." Written in 1940 and originally published in *The Objectivist*, it is the story of artistic integrity. While his mind naturally invents challenging, iconoclastic plots and characters, Henry Dorn tries to convince himself that "the simplest thing in the world" would be to compromise and give the public the old clichés it seems to want. However, for an artist, that proves too difficult. The story has a strong autobiographical strain as the critics misunderstand Henry Dorn's work in much the same way early critics missed the point in Rand's work. Dorn is also counseled, as Rand was, to be practical, to write what the public wants. He cannot, as Rand could not, which leaves him in an unresolved situation at the end of the story. Fortunately for us, Rand's story ended in triumph for herself and the public. The times proved that there is a large body of the public that wants to be challenged, that is hungry for ideals. A revised edition, which added the essay "Art and Cognition," was published in 1975.

THE NEW LEFT: THE ANTI-INDUSTRIAL REVOLUTION (1971)

Published in 1971, during the thick of the period that is called the sixties but lasted until the mid-seventies, this book's attacks on hippies and "smorgasbord education" seem dated. However, as Rand's predictions about the negative results of some of the practices she rails against come about, one begins to appreciate the perceptiveness of her logic. The specific audience for this book is college students and those who are concerned about them and modern education. Compiled and published in paperback at the suggestion of a graduate student, the work is seen by Rand as providing intellectual ammunition for students who seek a rational explanation for the activities of the New Left and the campus chaos left in their wake. The first essay, "Cashing-In: The Student 'Rebellion,' " was initially published in *The Objectivist Newsletter* and then in *Capitalism: The Unknown Ideal*. Except for one that was written for *The New York Times Magazine*, the rest of the articles were originally published in *The Objectivist*.

The most comprehensive of the articles included in this book is "The Comprachicos," a five-part chronicle of the destructive effects of American education. Rand begins with a translation from Victor Hugo's *The Man Who Laughs*, which describes a seventeenth-century association, the *comprachicos* (children buyers), which purposefully deformed children in order to create freaks that would be saleable as entertainment for courts and sideshows. She then develops the thesis that our progressive nursery schools begin an educational process that stunts the mind in a manner analagous to the way the *comprachicos* twisted the bodies of the hapless children that fell into their clutches. For Rand, the horror is compounded because "the *comprachicos* of the mind" do their mutilations openly. John Dewey receives censure in this indictment of the American educational system, as do the "look-see" technique of teaching reading that replaced phonetics and the discussion method of classroom teaching. "The Comprachicos" is a good illustration of Rand's predictive abilities. Her sweeping indictment of American education was called reactionary in its time, but today, her criticisms are in keeping with the conclusions of the President's Commission on Education.

In "The Anti-Industrial Revolution" Rand's analysis of the failure of old-line Marxism and the consequent support that new-line leftists give to anti-industrial and ecological movements provides food for thought. Since the promise of socialist abundance did not become a reality in Soviet Russia, Socialist Britain, or any other collectivist country, the new-line attack indicts capitalism for creating its abundance by denuding the landscape and polluting the environment. Of course, many of the adherents to the antinuclear, anti-industrial, and ecological movements are not leftists, but Rand's inferences about their utilization by anticapitalist propagandists are still valid.

Foretelling the bankruptcy of collectivist welfare states is another example of Rand's perceptiveness. It is not surprising that Margaret Thatcher, who turned around some of the negative effects of Britain's socialist policies, is an admirer of the writings of Ayn Rand. Rand's arguments for the life-expanding aspects of industrialization remind us, lest we become too enamored of an idyllic representation of the pastoral past, of the many ways our lives have benefited from the technological advances that we take for granted.

Since its original publication, this work has been notably revised several times. A second edition in 1975 added the essay "The Age of Envy." *Return of the Primitive: The Anti-Industrial Revolution*, published in 1999 and edited by Peter Schwartz, contains additional articles written by the editor in addition to the Rand essays from the 1975 edition.

INTRODUCTION TO OBJECTIVIST EPISTEMOLOGY (1979)

A theory of knowledge is basic to philosophy, and as all knowledge is acquired and stored in conceptual form, Rand chooses to introduce her theories on epistemology by presenting her theory of concepts. Before we can determine what we know, we must determine how concepts are formed, what their nature is, how we can ensure their validity. Although it was published in 1979, this book is composed wholly of materials originally published over a decade earlier in *The Objectivist*. Rand's original essays were also issued as a separate monograph of the same title by the Objectivist Book Service. In addition to Rand's eight-part essay, Leonard Peikoff's article, "The Analytic-Synthetic Dichotomy," which was also originally published in *The Objectivist*, is included. Rand begins with the axiom "Existence exists." By accepting that axiom, one acknowledges something exists that can be perceived and that one has a tool by which to perceive it (consciousness). "Existence exists" means that there is a reality independent of anyone's ability to perceive it. This is the core premise of philosophical Objectivism. Rand moves from that essential axiom to an explication of how one develops knowledge about that reality through sensations, percepts, and concepts. The importance of the mathematical process of measurement to the formation of concepts is explained, as are the processes of concept formation and the development of abstractions.

Special kinds of concepts such as concepts of consciousness and axiomatic concepts are also discussed. Rand explains that consciousness is experienced in relation to an external world. To be aware—to be conscious—is to be conscious of something. Consciousness has two attributes: content and action. Rand discusses the interrelationship of those two attributes at some length, distinguishing among concepts of cognition, concepts of method, and concepts of evaluation. Rand defines axiomatic concepts as those which identify a primary fact of reality, that is, those that cannot be reduced or broken down into smaller parts. Existence, identity, and consciousness are the fundamental axiomatic concepts; they cannot be proved and need no proof.

The special relationship of language to concept formation is discussed in the chapter on definitions. Rand's definition of language is "a code of visual-auditory symbols that serve the psycho-epistemological function of converting concepts into the mental equivalent of concretes." A definition, therefore, differentiates one concept from all other concepts as it identifies the distinguishing characteristics of the concept it defines. Rand credits Aristotle with being the first to formulate the principle of correct definitions. He believed, however, that definitions referred to metaphysical essences. It is on the issue of essences that Objectivism differs from Aristotle. Objectivism holds that the nature of essence is epistemological, not metaphysical. Rand differentiates Objectivism from the four schools of thought on the issue of concepts because it is the only philosophy that regards concepts as *objective*, derived from reality by the human mind, not revealed or invented.

A summary is provided at the end of the eight chapters. While it is useful, the subject matter is so abstruse, that unless one is well-versed in epistemology, I would not recommend relying on the summary.

Peikoff's "The Analytic-Synthetic Dichotomy" is a rebuttal of the prevailing philosophical contention that analytic truths are true simply because we say they are, logical argument being a subjective convention. Synthetic truths, then, are contingent, uncertain, and unprovable. Objectivism, which holds that "existence is a self-sufficient primary," rejects the metaphysical arguments of much of contemporary philosophy. An enlarged second edition includes excerpts from Rand's workshops on epistemology.

PHILOSOPHY: WHO NEEDS IT (1982)

Published posthumously, Ayn Rand's last projected anthology is introduced and organized by Leonard Peikoff, her literary heir. Rand was working on this book when she died. There is no new material in the book; most of the essays were originally published in *The Ayn Rand Letter*. The title article was first delivered as a graduation address at West Point.

Rand's premise, that everyone's action or inaction derives from a conscious or unconscious philosophy, is convincingly illustrated in a number of the preliminary essays. Rand uncovers the philosophical underpinnings for the beliefs and behavior of many contemporary intellectuals, as well as amoralists and those with "anti-conceptual" mentalities. She illustrates how the philosophies of Hume, Kant, Plato, James, and Emerson influence thinking even though, more often than not, the average individual is not aware of the source of such postulates as "Don't be so sure—nobody can be certain of anything," or "It may be true for you, but it is not true for me."

One of Rand's greatest gifts is her ability to cut to the heart of a contemporary event or issue and analyze its philosophical implications. The essay "Kant Versus Sullivan" is one example of Rand operating with that kind of critical clarity. Using the Broadway play *The Miracle Worker*, which is based on the true life account of how Annie Sullivan brought Helen Keller, who became both deaf and blind in infancy, into the realm of conceptual awareness, Rand cogently illustrates the undeniable significance of *the word*, of language. It is through the word that Helen is able to break out of her limited world of sensations and become a communicating part of the human family. Given that importance, Rand then castigates those acadamecians who publish articles that devalue the word and postulate "science without experience" and language without words.

THE AYN RAND LEXICON: OBJECTIVISM FROM A TO Z (1986)

Culling from the Objectivist corpus, editor Henry Binswanger creates a handy reference guide to Rand's philosophy, arranged by topic. Most of the material comes from Rand's nonfiction writing, although he does use those philosophical passages from the fiction that were reprinted in *For the New Intellectual*. Rand approved the project but saw only a small portion of it before she died.

THE VOICE OF REASON: ESSAYS IN OBJECTIVIST THOUGHT (1988)

Divided into three parts, Philosophy, Culture, and Politics, this anthology is composed of what editor Leonard Peikoff calls the "best of the non-anthologized Ayn Rand." Peikoff provides four essays in three sections and an Epilogue, "My Thirty Years with Ayn Rand: An Intellectual Memoir." The title page includes the information that there is an additional essay by Peter Schwartz. His contribution is "Libertarianism: The Perversion of Liberty."

AYN RAND'S MARGINALIA (1995)

A book of marginalia is by its very essence of problematic value. Interesting, yes, in the way that looking at the contents of people's medicine chests is. But it is of dubious value if one does not know the full context for all the prescriptions. In this collection, edited by Robert Mayhew, some of Rand's notes are extensive, especially when she is finding fault with a writer's basic premises. Although one is not surprised that Rand's comments are mostly negative, it is surprising that some of the harshest commentary is heaped on people who either were perceived as or thought themselves to be her allies or friends: John Hospers, Ludwig von Mises, F. A. Hayek, and Henry Hazlitt, in particular. Her comments, written in the margins of books by these men and others, provide some insight into her evaluation of what she read.

THE LETTERS OF AYN RAND (1995)

The uncommon variety of letters presented in this volume edited by Michael S. Berliner is but one of its values. The mix of letters allows the reader access to the many facets of Rand's private and public personae. Particularly warming is the insight into the Rand/O'Connor relationship provided by an early letter that begins "Cubby Sweet!" and is signed "Your Fluff." The letter is embellished with Rand's lion cub drawings. There are responses to fans, an extended correspondence with Frank Lloyd Wright, and even a letter that included recipes for beef stroganoff and salad dressing (too bad the editor did not publish the recipes). The volume ends with Rand's last letter, to her niece Mimi Sutton, wherein she enclosed a check to help with holiday expenses.

THE JOURNALS OF AYN RAND (1997)

In his editor's preface, David Harriman quotes Rand's admonition to herself: "From now on—no thought whatever about yourself, only about your work. You are only a writing engine." Among other things, this volume illustrates Rand's dedication to her craft and her meticulous preparation for writing. The term "journal," defined in this context as "her notes to herself through the decades," is imprecise since notes of a personal nature are excluded, saved for a forthcoming biography. Of particular interest are the scenarios that Rand wrote for the silent screen and the notes for her last projected novel "To Lorne Dieterling." Some of the early notes are translated from Russian. There is little material from the last decade and a half of her life.

RUSSIAN WRITINGS ON HOLLYWOOD (1999)

Two recent recoveries of Ayn Rand's earliest publications have been combined in *Russian Writings on Hollywood,* edited by Michael S. Berliner. One is a sixteen-page booklet on the actress Pola Negri, originally published by the Cinematographic Publishing House of the Russian Federation in 1925. The following year, *Hollywood: American City of Movies* was published. Readers are treated to facsimiles of both, followed by translations. Also included is a reproduction of Rand's movie diary, a listing of her ratings of various films and their actors and directors. The diary covers the period between 1922 and 1929.

THE OBJECTIVIST NEWSLETTER (January 1962– December 1965)

Edited and published by Ayn Rand and Nathaniel Branden, with Barbara Branden as managing editor and Elayne Kalberman as circulation manager, *The Objectivist Newsletter* includes articles and reviews by Barbara Branden, Alan Greenspan, Leonard Peikoff, Edith Efron, and Robert Hessen. Beatrice Hessen, Joan Blumenthal, Martin Anderson, and Joan Meltzer each contribute one review. The core of the newsletter, however, is provided by Rand and Branden. Most issues contain major commentary by each. The newsletter format provided for a front-page editorial essay, which dealt with some aspect of contemporary culture, politics, or ethics. The "Intellectual Ammunition Department" answered questions by readers in order to help them respond effectively to political and philosophical challenges to Objectivism. The "Books" section generally reviewed works of philosophy, history, and economics. (See the Appendix for a list of books favorably reviewed in Objectivist publications.) Occasionally a second article, either by a guest columnist or by either one of the editors who did not write the front-page essay, amplified an issue. The "Objectivist Calendar" provided information about publications, classes, lectures, readings, art shows, and even social events sponsored by the Nathaniel Branden Institute. The tone of these newsletters is exhilarating and self-confident. They exude a sense of accomplishment and excitement that is best exemplified in Nathaniel Branden's yearly "A Report to Our Readers," wherein the continuing progress of Objectivism is reviewed. In the December 1965 issue, Branden announces the transition to a magazine format for *The Objectivist.*

Rand and Branden cover a variety of subjects in their articles and "intellectual ammunition" responses. The first article in the first issue, "Check Your Premises," echoes a theme from *Atlas Shrugged.* In this article Rand warns all advocates of freedom about internal enemies that are more dangerous to our individual liberties than the threats from

Russia or any foreign country. The two culprits she names are the Federal Communications Commission (FCC) and Anti-Trust Laws. She denounces contemporary conservatives for having lost their philosophical base thus becoming reactors rather than actors. Rand points out that politics is but a branch of philosophy and that a consistent political theory is necessarily based on supporting metaphysics, epistemology, and ethics. Because of their basic philosophy, Objectivists are "radicals for capitalism," not conservatives.

Subsequent issues take up the questions of the FCC and Anti-Trust Laws. Rand calls antitrust "The Rule of Unreason." She points out the basic contradiction of "free competition" *enforced* by law. Antitrust laws function like a Catch-22; businesspeople can be prosecuted for prices that are too high, too low, or regulated. Businesspeople are the one group that distinguishes capitalism from totalitarianism. Their position is usurped by bureaucrats and commissars in collectivist states. If we value our freedom, we should fight for the rights of businesspeople. In her denunciation of Minow N. Minow, then chairman of the FCC, Rand explains the contradiction of allowing one man to decide what is in "the public interest." Minow had announced that any television or radio station that did not meet his criterion of public service would lose its license. The public expresses its interest by watching or listening to certain programs. If one person can decide that the public is not fit to judge its own interest, then cannot one person decide that the public is not competent to vote either, or to choose which products it should buy? Those who would protect us for our own good remove the basic freedom of choice. Rand then calls out for protection from our protectors, specifically big government, which, as it creates more and more bureaus and commissions to oversee our safety, plunges us deeper and deeper into debt, creates inflation, and interferes with our individual rights. Everyone is entitled to the same protection as consumers, Rand explains; therefore, if there are regulations protecting consumers from dishonesty on the part of manufacturers, should not politicians also be enjoined from marketing ideas that are hazardous to our health or life, from making misleading or mislabeled promises, from presenting a variety of programs whose hidden costs amount to a violation of truth in packaging?

The specific referents of these newsletters were events of the early sixties. What makes them intellectually satisfying today is that the basic premises Rand uses to criticize government, education, or literature apply now as they did then. When in "The Pull Peddlers" she decries the grotesquery of our citizens lobbying for special funds and favors for foreign governments, she could not have foretold the ultimate grotesquery of the brother of a president registering as the foreign agent of a country whose leader consistently denounces the United States (Billy Carter was a registered agent for the Libyan government). Such an episode would have been called exaggerated in *Atlas Shrugged*, but as Rand was to exclaim on another occasion, she had thought she was a Romantic writer; however, current events were proving her a Naturalist.

THE OBJECTIVIST (January 1966–September 1971)

Begun by Nathaniel Branden and Ayn Rand, with basically the same staff as *The Objectivist Newsletter*, *The Objectivist* is essentially the same matter but in different form. The May 1968 issue publishes Rand's explanation for the dissolution of all personal and professional relationships with both Nathaniel and Barbara Branden. Subsequent issues are edited by Rand with Leonard Peikoff as associate editor.

In June and July 1968, Rand printed "A Statement of Policy" which is her revision and redefinition of an earlier policy vis-à-vis students and supporters. Rand defines Objectivism as an intellectual movement with herself as its theoretician. Students and supporters are encouraged to study, discuss, and disseminate Objectivist ideas providing they do not attempt to act as "spokesmen for Objectivism." One of Rand's main concerns was with unannointed theoreticians who appropriated and then modified and otherwise twisted her philosophy. She delineates the only authentic sources: her own works; articles appearing in *The Objectivist* and *The Objectivist Newsletter*; books by authors endorsed by the Objectivist publications; *Who Is Ayn Rand?* and articles written by Nathaniel and Barbara Branden up to that time, but not in the future.

THE AYN RAND LETTER (October 1971–February 1976)

Published in a simple, typewritten letter format consisting of a fortnightly article by Rand, which was occasionally replaced with a piece by Leonard Peikoff, *The Ayn Rand Letter*'s only other feature is the "Objectivist Calendar."

There is abundant food for thought in the five years' worth of responses to national and international events. As always, Rand analyzes by boring to the underlying malignancy that causes the various symptoms she surveys. Whether it is a discussion of the disintegration of language or wage-price controls, she explains that the philosophy providing the underpinning for the majority of destructive contemporary activities is altruism, the moral base for collectivism. She also explains how irrationalism works as the epistemological base for both altruism and collectivism. Temporal events are predictable from the prevailing collectivist principles, and as Rand expounds over and over again, the battlefield must be philosophical. If one does not question the basic premises behind the issues, one cannot effectively fight them.

For those interested in U.S. presidential campaigns, there are a number of articles leading up to the Nixon–McGovern contest. Rand saw the Democratic National Convention of 1972 as the culmination of the collectivist track the party had been taking for forty years. Especially abhorrent to her was the platform promise to "make economic security a matter of right." In order to do that, Rand explains, those who produce must be enslaved to those who do not, and it is the worst kind of logical fallacy to base one person's rights on the destruction of another's. Another of McGovern's concepts that Rand deplores is his desire to effect a "redistribution of wealth." Such a plan is based on the premise that the wealth is his, or the government's, to distribute. Rand asks the relevant question: By what right would McGovern do so? A system where the government has such rights is communism. McGovern thought to use the income tax for such a purpose, but as Rand points out, this puts the burden on the productive who work. The beneficiaries of such a system are the rich, who do not have to work, and the nonproductive. Again, it is a matter of punishing the able for being able.

Among other issues that raise Rand's ire are the following: (1) government grants that have the effect of forcing citizens to support ideas they are vehemently opposed to, and (2) B. F. Skinner's theories, which Rand sees as eliminating the dignity of achievement by ascribing the differences in people to the type of reinforcement they received. One of the dangers of government grants is that when a government intrudes into the world of ideas in the form of subsidies, then the result can be a set of official ideas. As grants are given to "prestigious" researchers, this is a way of keeping those who are already part of the power establishment in power. As for Skinner, his utopian commune Twin Oaks, which could not subsist on its own, was supported by government money. In a two-part article, Rand repudiates Skinner's arguments, along with the American Philosophical Association for celebrating him, and even castigates the critics who gave his book *Beyond Freedom and Dignity* negative reviews for the wrong reasons.

Of particular interest to those who agree with much of what Rand has to say, but do not know how to help propagate her theories, is her 1972 response to the question "What Can One Do?" Her answer is that since the battle is philosophical, an intellectual battle is necessary. Minds must be convinced. Beginning with the self and not expecting to influence too large a group are two starting instructions. It is important to develop one's own consistent philosophy so that one can deal with challenges and questions. Rand cautions against joining the wrong ideological groups because they seem to espouse views with which one agrees while their fundamental principles conflict with much that one believes in. Examples she gives are the Libertarians and conservative parties. Ad hoc committees she finds acceptable because they usually have but one goal.

Above all, Rand counsels people to speak out. Speak out against the irrational. Do not keep silent.

In November 1975, Ayn Rand announced that she would have to cease publication of *The Ayn Rand Letter*. The *Letter* had fallen behind schedule. The August 1974 issue had been written in May 1975, at which time Rand announced that she would change the fortnightly schedule to a monthly format. However, even that was too burdensome. In "A Last Survey," she carefully and explicitly outlines for her readers her reasons for discontinuance. The wonder is not that at the age of seventy she was quitting an onerous schedule of bimontly or monthly philosophical articles along with all the other obligations she faced; the wonder is that for fourteen years she was able to supply the various newsletters with a steady stream of philosophical responses to events of the times.

CHAPTER 5

Criticism of Rand's Works

Ayn Rand was a polemical writer; therefore, it is not surprising that her works often arouse heated reaction from a variety of sources. There are some who vilify her, even now after her death; the adjective "fascist" comes easily to the tongues of those on the left. There are others who idolize her; she had many disciples in her lifetime, and students of Objectivism have been curiously blind to any imperfections in the articulator of the philosophy. Blind adoration and faith in Rand's precepts are so often characteristic of her followers that the word "cult" is routinely applied to Rand's adherents. One of the critical works that will be discussed in this chapter asks the pointed question: "Is Objectivism a Religion?" Another work to be examined is titled *The Ayn Rand Cult*.

Rand disciples are unfazed by accusations of zealotry and lack of critical perspective. Leonard Peikoff's response to such charges is that being uncompromising purists is exactly what Rand would have wanted Objectivists to be.[1] The writings of those associated with or sanctioned by The Ayn Rand Institute reflect that position. As Rand broke with many one-time associates during her lifetime over what she considered deviations from her values, so her designated heirs are also prone to suspicion of any deviance from their closely monitored fundamentalism. It is not surprising then, that in the years since her death, Objectivism has been fractured by a division between the orthodox, which has control of Rand's estate and papers, and those who, although they consider Rand "the most eloquent spokesman in our time for the values of reason, achievement, individualism, and freedom," call for more open discussion and debate of her ideas. The Institute for Objectivist Studies, founded by David Kelley, is the catalyst for the dissident group.

There are other venues for Rand criticism. *Full Context* represents itself as an "An International Objectivist Publication." The journal *Objectivity* publishes articles from a Rand-inspired perspective. There are also a large number of present and former admirers among the members of various Libertarian organizations and institutes. The Cato Institute co-sponsored the 40th anniversary celebration of the publication of *Atlas Shrugged*. Primarily Libertarian publications, such as *Liberty* and *Reason*, routinely feature articles about Rand and Objectivism. Politically, Rand is an anomaly; she antagonizes and attracts liberals and conservatives, equally. She is most appealing to those who follow no party line.

During Rand's lifetime, the preponderance of critical response fell into the camp of either supporter or antagonist. Since her death, another element has been added to the mix of mostly polemic critical reactions. Scholarly works that are neither adulatory nor derisive, but that seek to evaluate Rand's fiction and philosophy as part of the ongoing give and take of academic dialogue are a growing part of the critical mix. A few independent scholars, allied with neither of the aforementioned groups have sought to engage Rand's works from a variety of perspectives, often in the context of their role in the history of ideas.

Ironically, although orthodox Randians name, as one of their goals, a heightened receptivity to Objectivism in universities, they have not been overly responsive to requests by university scholars for information or access.[2] This is unfortunate, since the scholarly works issued so far with the sanction of the Rand estate have not always exhibited a confidence-inspiring level of academic rigor. Bibliography, which is a significant indicator of the depth and breadth of research, is self-referential or else nonexistent. The *Ayn Rand Lexicon* eschews ellipses as "clutter."[3] The *Letters of Ayn Rand* publishes an incorrect birth date in the chronology of Rand's life.[4] With no explanation, the *Journals of Ayn Rand* publishes a different version of a Rand journal entry than was published earlier in *The Objectivist Forum*.[5] One gets the sense that works sanctioned by the Rand estate are strictly in-house operations. Quality critical publication gains from refereeing and editing by neutral professionals. Academic credibility is established by the discipline of review by disinterested evaluators. That is why articles and books submitted to scholarly journals and presses are subject to blind peer review.

One of the purposes of this chapter is to annotate the major critical works. Another is to present the gist of the different critical perspectives offered in more concentrated venues, most especially those published in newspapers, magazines, and journals. Rand's impact, however, is not limited to expression in either the mass media or academic journals. The broad impact of her influence manifests itself in a variety of ways. A character drawn from her theories is the hero of an arcane comic book;[6] a contemporary rock group dedicated an album to her spirit;[7] Rand appears as character or in the theme of several novels.[8] A quotation from *Anthem* inspired a trio for piano, violin, and violoncello.[9]

Rand's arguments are provocative. The pictures she creates of the ills and monsters of contemporary society appeal to our frustrations with a government that has mushroomed out of control and personal vistas that seem increasingly circumscribed. The strength of her arguments and the attraction of her solutions are convincing reasons to consider her explanations for what has gone awry and her prescriptions for treating a variety of contemporary maladies. During her lifetime, hers seemed to be a voice crying out alone against the prevailing *zeitgeist* of political and economic collectivism. In recent decades, her jeremiads have proven prophetic.

After World War II and the defeat of one type of totalitarian collectivism, fascism, the United States found itself locked in a cold war with another, communism. Even our staunchest allies adopted collectivist governments and economies of one form or another. One can see why Rand would have been depressed by what she perceived as the direction of the world around her. Much has changed, however, since the earlier edition of this book, which was published only two years after her death. The political and economic culture of our country and of much of the world has altered in a way that makes it more receptive to her ideas. Communist and collectivist governments and economies have proven ineffectual in the global marketplace. The rationality, if not the morality, of Rand's championship of capitalism has won the day. Contemporary mentions of her routinely acknowledge her impact on current political, economic, philosophical, and psychological mores. This is in marked contrast to the derision to which she was subjected in her lifetime.

The strength of her impact and the validity of her ideas make it important to weigh and evaluate the critiques of both supporters and detractors. Her philosophy demands it; one of her major messages is that, in all cases, one must use independent judgment. It is hoped that the synopses that follow will help readers in those evaluations, presenting positive and negative reactions, both the thoughtful and the vituperative.

The basis for the following synopses is the complete listing in Parts II and III in the Bibliography of all the books, articles, and reviews of Rand's works, as well as the references to her that I read in the preparation of the original *Ayn Rand Companion* and this updated and revised edition. Readers can use the Bibliography as a basic resource if they wish to study further or evaluate for themselves. The following discussions are synoptic, not comprehensive, the purpose being to give a sense of the kinds of criticism and reviews that Rand's works elicited. Therefore, not every single work of criticism, positive or negative, is mentioned— only certain illustrative pieces. Although I expect readers will want to make their own evaluations of the efficacy of the criticism, on occasion I have pointed out some of the more obvious critical biases and inconsistencies.

Book-length studies will be summarized individually. The books are arranged chronologically. Bibliographical essays about articles and essays follow the book summaries.

BOOKS

Who Is Ayn Rand? (1962)
by Nathaniel Branden and Barbara Branden

The first full-length work to be published about Ayn Rand was written by her disciples and partners in the dissemination of Objectivist philosophy. For nearly two decades, that nineteen-year period in which Rand's literary star blazed brightest during her lifetime, the Brandens were her closest associates. *Who Is Ayn Rand?* both benefits and suffers from that close perspective. On the plus side, Barbara Branden's biographical essay, a response to the title question, provides the only personally authorized memoir of the life of a woman who was very secretive about her private life and history. The Brandens did not know even Rand's full real name until Barbara Branden unearthed it in the research for her biography.

Nathaniel Branden's essays about Rand's literary methodology, the implications of her philosophy for psychology, and the detailed analysis "The Moral Revolution in *Atlas Shrugged*," are synoptic and illuminating. As an authorized vita, however, *Who Is Ayn Rand?* is guilty of the limitations of that genre: only that which Rand approved is included. Nathaniel Branden has since repudiated the book publicly and in print. In 1971, he expressed the wish that the book had never been written: "If it were possible to prevent its further distribution, I would do so," he claimed in a 1971 interview with *Reason* magazine.[10] In subsequent interviews, he has softened his stand, allowing the value of some of the essays on her literary methods.

Barbara Branden has also stated that although the material presented in her biographical essay was written in good faith, the portrait of Rand that it develops is one-sided and does not represent the total picture.[11]

Is Objectivism a Religion? (1968)
by Albert Ellis

Albert Ellis readily identifies himself as an opponent of Objectivism. In fact, this book resulted from his inability to complete his "objections to Objectivism" within the time frame and strictures of a public debate between himself and Nathaniel Branden. Ellis not only finds fault with Objectivism's claim to rationality, but he also indicts it as detrimental to the psychological well-being of its practitioners. Ellis's main thesis is that

Objectivism, for all its claims of rationality, is a religion; his methodology is to enumerate the ten characteristics of "true believers" and then to illustrate how Objectivists exemplify those qualities to a lesser or greater degree.

Like most critics, Ellis is best at fault finding. His arguments also suffer from an obvious self-serving bias: He is promoting his own rational-emotive psychotherapy. Another deficiency in Ellis's criticism is his lack of standards. While Rand and Branden work from a value hierarchy, Ellis refuses to judge. In his system, even the individual who is "wrong, mistaken, and irresponsible," and who *chooses* to commit wrong deeds, need not be condemned. Curiously, however, while Ellis is careful not to convict wrongdoers, he is quick to condemn Rand.

His techniques, too often, are name calling and circular argument. His response to Rand's claim that the best product at the cheapest price would win in the marketplace is "this is arrant hogwash, as virtually any reasonably intelligent high school student of economics should be able to see."[12]

While this kind of posturing is dramatic, it rests on a logical fallacy taught in most freshman English texts. To Ellis's credit, he goes on to explain how Rand's statement does not take into account vagaries of the marketplace, such as fads and consumers who might not be rational. "Sheer drivel," he exclaims on one page; "Balderdash," he cries on the next. Although such opening ripostes as "What claptrap!" tend to detract from the serious character of his criticism, he does follow such flippancies with some salient observations about aspects of capitalism and human nature that Rand ignores.

The most telling argument for the aptness of Ellis's criticisms came shortly after his book was published. Following his "excommunication," Nathaniel Branden made statements that corroborate the validity of some of Ellis's arguments. In an interview with *Reason* magazine, Branden explains that his book *The Disowned Self* is, among other things, an attempt to undo the damage he had done to students of Objectivism by inadvertently encouraging them to distrust their emotions.[13] His statement lends credence to Ellis's opinion that Objectivism had a strong negative effect on the emotional health of its devotees. Ellis also excoriates Objectivists for being too judgmental and intolerant; rather than wanting to understand wrongdoers, he says, they want "to ruthlessly squelch, persecute, annihilate them." Ellis refers to Rand's hostility and anger when questioned in a way she did not find suitable. Branden acknowledges that in the early days of the movement, he too had treated questioners too harshly, but that as his attitude changed, he tried to harness Rand's cruel treatment of unfortunates who antagonized her.

Much of the fun of reading Ellis results from his verbal high jinks. It is a pleasure similar to the one derived from extravagant satire; one is amused by the exaggeration. However, occasionally, the same extravagance and exaggeration detract from the serious nature of the arguments.

With Charity Toward None (1971)
by William F. O'Neill

This book is the first evenhanded book dealing with Rand's philosophies. William F. O'Neill has no axe to grind as Ellis does, nor is he a crusader as John W. Robbins is. O'Neill's is a reasonable, detailed analysis of the validity of the basic philosophical propositions of Objectivism. His purpose is to answer two questions: (1) Are Rand's principles rational (valid/consistent) with themselves? (2) Are they true empirically?

O'Neill's methodology is to examine Rand's precepts by an "as objective as possible" application of the scientific verification process. Although his critique is generally negative and he finds Rand "guilty of occasional inconsistencies, contradictions and ambiguities," he also expresses admiration for Rand's intellectual and moral courage. O'Neill appreciates Rand's importance as "a useful intellectual catalyst in a society which frequently suffers from philosophical 'tired blood.' "[14]

In O'Neill's evaluation, Rand asks the right questions even if she postulates the wrong answers. He is especially approving of the fact that she has provoked so many people into thinking.

It Usually Begins with Ayn Rand (1972)
by Jerome Tuccille

Jerome Tuccille has the appealing quality of being able to laugh at himself. He also manages to poke fun at everyone else. Only the first two chapters of this book are about Rand, specifically; the rest of the book is a wild and wacky journey through the confusion of right-wing politics. The book is subtitled "A Libertarian Odyssey."

Like other critics, Tuccille notes contradictions in Rand's application of her own philosophy. He is particularly devastating in his satire of Objectivist cabals at Rand's apartment. Tuccille points out the irony in the Communist-style purges of those who did not toe the Rand line, since Rand was such a vehement opponent of communism. Rand negated her own principles of rationality and individualism by not allowing any deviation from her interpretation of reality. He calls Objectivism "a wonderfully appealing religion substitute."

Answer to Ayn Rand: A Critique of the Philosophy of Objectivism (1974)
by John W. Robbins

In *Answer to Ayn Rand*, John W. Robbins does not pretend objectivity; his stated purpose is "to correct a new and growing movement in America." He describes his thesis straightforwardly.

> The argument of this book will be destructive; it will attempt to demonstrate that Objectivism is self-contradictory, that its epistemology must lead to skepticism, its metaphysics to the void, its ethics to hedonism, and its politics to anarchy.[15]

Robbins is most effective in delineating inconsistencies in Objectivism, but his arguments are often naive or ignorant. For example, he accuses Rand of smuggling a great deal of Christianity into Objectivism. What he either fails to understand or does not know is that the ideas he accuses her of lifting existed prior to the birth and practice of Christianity. The archetype of the hero/savior leading a select and elect group to a utopia is certainly not a Christian exclusive.

In the initial section of the book, Robbins unfolds a well-argued, logical critique. Unfortunately, in other sections logic is abandoned. In the discussion of metaphysics, Robbins's frame of reference is made clear. Robbins does not believe in reason; he is a champion of revelation. His book is a response to Rand in the name of Jesus Christ. What he is doing is proselytizing for Christianity as the only basis for a free and stable society.

The Philosophic Thought of Ayn Rand (1984)
edited by Douglas J. Den Uyl and Douglas B. Rasmussen

This book by Douglas J. Den Uyl and Douglas B. Rasmussen is a major contribution to Rand scholarship. Its significance is underscored by a number of factors. Not only was it the first book about Rand to be published after a ten-year hiatus, but it was completed after her death and therefore has the benefit of dealing with a relatively complete corpus of her work.

Den Uyl and Rasmussen clarify their intention, which is "to evaluate Rand according to the same scholarly standards that would apply to any philosopher."[16] They also seek to move the discussion of Rand out of the range of the personal and into the realm of serious scholarship. One of the ongoing complaints of Rand students and admirers has been the refusal of "intellectuals" to accord her serious attention. The fact that a university press published this book is an important factor in its effectiveness in initiating attention in academic circles. In order "to maintain a consistent level of professional standards," the editors have collected a group of essays by academicians who are also acknowledged thinkers in their own right.

The anthology is divided into three sections: Metaphysics, Ethics, and Politics. Each section begins with an interpretive essay by Den Uyl and Rasmussen in which they explain Rand's basic hypotheses in each of these three fields. Following their introductory pieces are critical essays by Wallace Matson and Robert Hollinger in the area of metaphysics; Jack Wheeler, J. Charles King, and Eric Mack in the ethics section; and Antony Flew and Tibor R. Machan on politics. The essays are perceptive and enlightening. They are marked by a willingness to acknowledge the validity of some of Rand's contentions while pointing out what the individual authors consider to be gaps in her knowledge and errors in her thinking. More important, they are an essential element in ensuring that her ideas will be perpetuated. As Wallace Matson so tellingly explains, "Intellectual progress is inextricably bound up with critical give-and-take."[17] The only alternative to critical dialogue is stagnation.

While the quality of these essays is impressive, some are more available to the lay reader than others. As all the contributors are philosophers, writing in an academic press, terminology and allusions that are commonplace for them are not readily comprehensible to those outside of the discipline. For those, however, who are serious in their desire to see Rand's philosophy subjected to critical analysis, the study is well worth the effort.

The Passion of Ayn Rand (1986)
by Barbara Branden

A generation after her first turn as Ayn Rand's official biographer, Barbara Branden attempts to transcend the pain of their ruptured relationship and write about Rand with some perspective and objectivity. Her biography benefits from numerous interviews and indefatigable research (she even called Rand's sister in St. Petersburg) enhanced by the vantage point of first-hand knowledge. Seasoning and distance also help. Among Branden's advantages as a biographer is the fact that she was able to use some fifty hours of taped interviews made for the earlier biographical essay. These tapes are unusual in that Rand speaks of her early years, not a habit of the woman who re-created herself when she came to this country.

Branden accomplishes a rare feat for biographers; she is able to illuminate both the attractive and repellent components of Rand's personality, showing why so many would follow her unreservedly, while others reacted with abhorrence. The most sensational aspect of Branden's book is the first public acknowledgment of that which had only been whispered of before: Ayn Rand's extramarital affair with Nathaniel Branden and the resultant rupture when he hid from Rand the fact that he had fallen in love with another woman. "The break" with the Brandens pitted friend against friend, family against family. Leonard Peikoff, Barbara's cousin, replaced the Brandens as Rand's literary heir. In light of the vituperative nature of the split, Branden's work is a remarkably balanced biography. As one would expect, the reviewers reflect the continuing animosities created by the original rupture.

Branden's admiration for and desire to understand Rand predominate, although she does not refrain from confronting the more unpleasant qualities of her subject. As she says in her introduction: "Those who worship Ayn Rand and those who damn her do her the same disservice: They make her unreal and they deny her humanity. I hope to show in her story that she was something infinitely more fascinating and infinitely more valuable than either goddess or sinner. She was a human being. She lived, she loved, she fought her battles and knew triumph and defeat. The scale was epic."[18]

Ayn Rand (1987)
by James T. Baker

James T. Baker's volume in the Twayne's United States Authors Series generally follows the pattern of the first edition of *The Ayn Rand Companion*, although the chapters are more amply named. "Biographical Data" becomes "The Life and Times of Ayn Rand"; "The Fiction" becomes "Ayn Rand as Creative Writer." Although Baker claims to want to rescue Rand from the hands of both her admirers and detractors and give her a fair and objective assessment, his treatment of her fiction and philosophy is often tinged with that cavalier dismissal with which he admittedly first assessed her work.

Judgment Day: My Years with Ayn Rand (1989)
by Nathaniel Branden

Judgment Day is, as the title suggests, not Rand's story, but that of Nathaniel Branden. While *The Passion of Ayn Rand*, by Branden's former wife, Barbara, is a biography of Rand, dependent on research to give form to that part of Rand's life that Barbara Branden was wholly absent from, *Judgment Day* is a memoir of a relationship, more limited in its vision of Rand and more dependent on the author's memory. Why, then, one might ask, is it included in this criticism chapter? The answer, of course, is that it presents Rand from the perspective of one who knew her in a way no one else did. Whatever disagreements one might have with Nathaniel Branden's presentation of the facts as he remembers them, he was, in a very real way, both a midwife and a founder of the Objectivist movement. It was through his organization, the Nathaniel Branden Institute, that Objectivism was first spread to eager students in this country. For those who do not hew to the orthodox Objectivist line, Nathaniel Branden remains a significant figure. He has created a career for himself, independent of his association with Rand.

In Defense of Ayn Rand (1990)
by Virginia L. L. Hamel

Ayn Rand could not respond to the representation of the darker aspects of her behavior presented in Barbara Branden's *The Passion of Ayn Rand*, Murray Rothbard's "The Sociology of the Ayn Rand Cult," and Nathaniel Branden's *Judgment Day* and "Passages Cut from Judgment Day." On behalf of Rand, Virginia L. L. Hamel presents a point-by-point defense, buttressed by research into legal documents, some first-hand observation, and a reasoned reading of Rand's perspective. Hamel's research includes previously unpublished public records, such as the official report of Patrecia Gullison Branden's death, the terms of the Branden divorce settlement, and subsequent legal battles. She takes particular issue with the fact that the works by Rothbard and both Brandens were all published after Rand's death, thereby leaving Rand unable to confront her enemies.

Hamel saves her harshest criticisms for Nathaniel Branden, who she sees as a slick self-salesman, using his skills as a psychotherapist to manipulate the reader. She calls his book, *Judgment Day*, among other things, an instrument of revenge against his ex-wife Barbara, saying that even those who dislike her "are shocked at the degree of his brutality toward her."[19] For Hamel, *Judgment Day* is unforgivable as a "memoir which lays open the personal life of a very fine and private woman [Rand] for public entertainment and personal profit."

Objectivism: The Philosophy of Ayn Rand (1991)
by Leonard Peikoff

Rand's articulation of her philosophy was organic, evolving over a period of years, first through the medium of her fiction and then periodically in articles and books. Leonard Peikoff identifies his book as "the first comprehensive statement of her philosophy."[20] He acknowledges, however, that he has rewritten much of the lecture material that Rand originally authorized as consonant with her philosophy. He excuses his lack of documentation by claiming that "where no reference is given, the material in all likelihood is taken from the lengthy philosophical discussion that I had with Miss Rand across a period of decades."[21]

The reader who wants a comprehensive view of orthodox Objectivism as it has evolved since Rand's death should start with Peikoff's book. His thorough coverage runs from chapter one on "Reality" through chapter twelve on "Art," with an epilogue on the duel between Plato and Aristotle.

The Ideas of Ayn Rand (1991)
by Ronald E. Merrill

Ronald E. Merrill writes from the perspective of a nostalgic participant in the early Objectivist movement. Merrill met Rand but was not one of her inner circle. He is neither an Objectivist fundamentalist nor a heretic; still he discounts much that has been written about the cultic aspects of early Objectivism. Blaming both Rand and her inner circle for the cult of personality that eventually led to what he calls "the Great Schism," he refuses to "judge the ideas by the personality of the thinker."[22] He can and does appreciate her genius, while not hesitating to point out the flaws or errors in her judgment. Merrill is judiciously adroit at tracing the development of Rand's intellectual growth through the projection of her ideas in her creative writing, particularly the transition from a strongly Nietzschean inclination to a developing Objectivism.

Atheism, Ayn Rand, and Other Heresies (1991)
by George H. Smith

Although it is properly only partially about Ayn Rand, George H. Smith's book, in part, like Jerome Tucille's It Usually Begins with Ayn Rand, traces a personal intellectual odyssey that was greatly affected by Rand.[23] Even if, as Smith explains, he eventually "experienced an abrupt deconversion from orthodox Randianism," he credits Rand with the important contribution of convincing him, and countless other young people, "that ideas matter."[24]

In his discussion, he credits Rand's epistemological argument for atheism as being one of the strongest, distinguishing features of Objectivism. With her theory of knowledge as a philosophical underpinning, Objectivist atheism is able to withstand charges of nihilism and pessimism. Smith's chapter "Ayn Rand: Philosophy and Controversy" contributes a detailed comparison between Rand's philosophical ideas and those of a variety of other thinkers. Finally, he addresses the paradox of Objectivism as a religion. Smith's book contextualizes Rand's thought within the framework of various contemporary heresies, or challenges, to orthodox ways of thinking.

Ayn Rand: The Russian Radical (1995)
by Chris Matthew Sciabarra

Chris Matthew Sciabarra's contribution to Rand studies lies in the originality of his approach, an approach which locates Rand's thought within the prevailing intellectual streams of her native Russia. He theorizes that, despite her protestations to the contrary, Rand may have absorbed much from the prevailing currents in Russian art and education, especially from the dialectic approaches of Hegelians and Marxists. He shows this through an impressive job of research, which involved a study of Russian Silver Age writers and the tracking down of Rand's university records and the relatives of her professor, N. O. Lossky. Although there has been challenge to some of his inductive leaps, Sciabarra's work is a significant milestone in Rand studies, placing her in the context of intellectual history.

The Stance of Atlas: An Examination of the
Philosophy of Ayn Rand (1997)
by Peter Erickson

Peter Erickson's format is both traditional and original. Harking back to Greek philosophical methodology, he presents his chapters in the form of dialogues. While traditional, this format is also original in that criticism is rarely written in this way any more and certainly no other book about Rand uses this device. Erickson credits Rand, who presented her philosophy through the medium of characters in novels, with being the inspiration for his methodology.

Three characters, Dr. Stanford, Doxa, and Penelope are joined by a fourth, Philosophus, Erickson's spokesperson. Their meetings, taking place over a period of fourteen days, are divided into discussions of different aspects of Rand's philosophy, including perception, the conceptual level of consciousness, axioms, facts and universals, and free will. Both strengths and weaknesses are explicated, so the reader can judge the validity of the various arguments. Finally, Erickson, who counts Rand as one of his philosophical antecedents, introduces his own philosophy, Factivity.

Without a Prayer: Ayn Rand and the Close of Her
System (1997)
by John W. Robbins

Much more blatantly than in his earlier book, *Answer to Ayn Rand*, where his religious position was not revealed until late in the text, John W. Robbins immediately declares his intention of replying to Rand in the name of Jesus Christ. He also presents a writer he wants people to read instead of Rand, one Gordon Haddon Clark, whose history of philosophy, *Thales to Dewey*, was published the same year as *Atlas Shrugged*. A good part of the book, however, is used to demonstrate the "errors of Objectivism."[25] Basic to Robbins's analysis is the premise that "reason is and must always be the handmaid of faith."[26] Robbins clarifies his scriptural position vis-à-vis both his philosophy and Rand's. He claims he will address only her precisely defined Objectivist canon as it stood in 1968, but he does go on to take some broad swipes at Leonard Peikoff and David Kelley in the Appendix. Peikoff's *The Ominous Parallels* is dismissed in less than two and a half pages as a work of desipience. In his attack on *The Evidence of the Senses*, Robbins grants that Kelley is a "very good" writer but accuses him of transforming Rand's quasi-Aristotelian epistemology into a quasi-Kantianism.

How does Robbins account for the power of what he calls Rand's "lethal system of ideas"?[27] The packaging is all, he says. It is her "literary ability—her narrative power, her eloquence and her rhetoric" which convince, not her logic.[28]

Ayn Rand: A Sense of Life (1998)
by Michael Paxton

This photographic and biographic companion to Michael Paxton's documentary film of the same title is beautifully produced and engaging in and of itself, whether or not one has seen the film. The pictures of Rand, in both her playful and professional stances, are priceless. Paxton had access to The Ayn Rand Institute (ARI) archives and includes rare photos of Rand as a child with her family, including a pin-up style picture of her sister Nora with her colorful imaginings of a glamorous world. Notable also is Paxton's investigative acumen in tracking down stills of Rand in the crowd scenes of Cecil B. De Mille's *King of Kings*.

As an "authorized" biographer, Paxton had to accede to certain stipulations and review by Rand's estate; that is usually the case for "authorized" biographers—only positive material is included. But whatever one may think about the lack of balance in his documentary and book, the book provides the reader with the unduplicable experience of access to Ayn Rand's own treasure trove of memorabilia.

The Fountainhead: An American Novel (1998)
by Douglas Den Uyl

Douglas Den Uyl's convincing reading of *The Fountainhead* as "the quintessential presentation of American individualism, American optimism, and the promise that is America" is important not only for its clear-headed and persuasive development of that thesis, but also because its inclusion in the Twayne's Masterwork Studies series marks a watershed in Rand scholarship. *The Fountainhead* thereby achieves a canonical status, putting it in the same category as *The Great Gatsby*, *Huckleberry Finn*, and *The Grapes of Wrath*.

Den Uyl's discussion, in a chapter called "Characters as Ideas," of how Rand melds art and philosophy is lucid and instructive, providing food for thought to both the innocent and sophisticated reader of this novel. His other chapters are equally insightful. Whether or not one agrees with all of his assessments, one can acknowledge that in terms of his thesis, which posits individualism as central to Americanism, Den Uyl justifies his reading of *The Fountainhead* as the "great American novel."

My Years with Ayn Rand: The Truth Behind the Myth (1998)
by Nathaniel Branden

Although it covers basically the same material as *Judgment Day*, this newly revised version benefits from the emotional and intellectual distance of the dozen years since the original was published. In his own words, Nathaniel Branden seeks to present "a more balanced portrait," correct some minor factual errors, and eliminate or revise passages that "contained unintended and misleading implications." Both tone and structure contribute to that end in this retelling of a story of high drama and tragic ironies.

The Ayn Rand Cult (1999)
by Jeff Walker

Jeff Walker's title telegraphs his tone. He contends that Ayn Rand's ideas are "conducive to cultishness" and that his research uncovered "a classic cult phenomenon." However, the methodology he uses to argue his theses is questionable and often depends on innuendo, rather than logic. In one instance he writes: "While the cult that formed around Ayn Rand didn't lead to Jonestown, Solar Temple, or Heaven's Gate–style mayhem—very few cults do—suicides, murderous motives, and death threats *have* been associated with it."[29] There is no proof here, just guilt by association. In the service of his comparison, he invokes horrible instances of mass hysteria, cases where people killed themselves or were killed. But, he does not provide one instance of a suicide or murder related to Ayn Rand. The trouble with this kind of overstatement is that it undercuts his valid arguments about the negative effects of too strict adherence to Objectivism. Much of his text is culled from his 1991–92 interviews with a number of key people in the movement who provide ample illustrations.

Walker proclaims that Barbara Branden's biography, Nathaniel Branden's memoir, and Chris Sciabarra's explication of Rand's Russian roots add some, but "not much" understanding of Ayn Rand and her movement.[30] In an effort to prove that Rand is derivative, Walker discusses works Rand did not read and includes repetition of unfounded gossip. If firsthand accounts and massive research add little, it is unlikely that Walker's techniques will add much. His hypothesis that Alisa Rosenbaum chose the name Rand because it would ring bells for most Jews due to its association with the South African "rand" is not only dependent on an anachronism, but also smacks of anti-Semitism. There is material of interest here, but one has to pick through a lot of muck to get at it.

Feminist Interpretations of Ayn Rand (1999)
edited by Mimi Reisel Gladstein and Chris Matthew Sciabarra

This volume gives evidence of the global impact of Rand's ideas. It contains essays by such diverse voices as an independent scholar in Norway, a literature professor in Australia, and a linguistics professor in France. A number of the contributors are part of mainstream academia. Many, however, are not. As is fitting in a balanced anthology, there is no conformity of thought. Of significance in the context of the acceptance of Rand's place in twentieth-century thought is the fact that, like the 1984 anthology *The Philosophical Thought of Ayn Rand* by Douglas J. Den Uyl and Douglas B. Rasmussen, it is published by a prestigious university press. It is part of a series that rereads the works of such canonical thinkers as Aristotle, Plato, Friedrich Nietzsche, Hannah Arendt, Mary Wollstonecraft, and Simone de Beauvoir.

Ayn Rand (forthcoming)
by Tibor Machan

In the preface to what he calls an introduction of Ayn Rand's ideas to a broader readership, Tibor Machan reminds readers that many important thinkers such as Marx, Nietzsche, Freud, and Sartre attracted ardent followers and disciples. But, Machan's purpose in this work is to explore the ideas, not the nature of their promulgation. This he does in a number of chapters that focus on Rand's understanding of axiomatic concepts and propositions, the basis for her epistemology, her moral philosophy of ethical egoism, and her social philosophy of rational individualism.

Chapters entitled "Rand versus Marx" and "Rand's Moriarty" follow. In the former, Machan explores the nature of Rand's anti-Marxism on grounds of individualism and capitalism. Rand's Moriarty, or archenemy, is identified as Immanuel Kant; the basis of Rand's detestation, as clarified by Machan, rests on the philosopher's devastating critique of human reason. Machan's final chapter outlines areas of Rand's philosophy that, according to the chapter title, still have "room for work."

More books are forthcoming. *What Art Is: The Esthetic Theory of Ayn Rand* by Louis Torres and Michelle Marder Kamhi grows out of their co-authored articles that appeared serially in *Aristos*. Set for a 1999 publication date, it promises a comprehensive investigation of Rand's premises in the context of other esthetic theories as well as such fields as archaeology, anthropology, ethnomusicology, neurology, and psychology. My own volume for Twayne's Masterworks Studies, tentatively titled *Atlas Shrugged: Manifesto of the Mind*, is in progress.

ARTICLES

Many of the articles written about Ayn Rand's novels are concerned with the effects of her ideas on her readers. The strength of her appeal both amazes and frightens her detractors. In *The New York Times Book Review* silver anniversary article about *The Fountainhead*, "A Strange Kind of Simplicity," Nora Ephron promises herself never to read the book again, although she professes to "still have a great affection for it and [would] recommend it to anyone taking a plane trip." Ephron remembers being deeply affected by the book when she first read it at eighteen, but in retrospect calls, what she describes as, "the most astonishing phenomenon in publishing history" a silly book and claims that the young are fascinated by *The Fountainhead* because they miss the point.[31]

After cataloging Rand's deficiencies as both writer and public persona, Barbara Grizzuti Harrison muses about the bases of Rand's attraction for so many women in her 1978 article "Psyching Out Ayn Rand." Harrison's conclusion is that the appeal is largely due to the power of the fantasy of a strong, dominant woman who is overpowered by an even stronger and more dominant male who is yet willing to lay all of his power at the feet of the heroine. Harrison is appalled and theorizes that narcissism, low self-esteem, and the appeal of selfishness after a lifetime of traditionally feminine sacrificial behavior account for Rand's appeal to the female psyche. Harrison admits that Rand's appeal includes men, particularly the middle class; she accuses Rand of pandering to their fears. Harrison concludes, "I am afraid of Ayn Rand."[32] This essay is reprinted in *Feminist Interpretations of Ayn Rand*.

Like Harrison, Bruce Cook is fearful of Rand's influence. Writing as both a Catholic and a liberal, Cook, in "Ayn Rand: A Voice in the Wilderness" (1965), is seriously concerned with Rand's ability "to attract adolescents and the Far Right." He views her lack of charity and contempt for religion as damaging for her followers. More than once, he makes allusions that compare her theories to fascism.[33]

John Kobler, more bemused at Rand's appeal than concerned for the souls of her adherents, is not as condemnatory as Cook. In his "Curious Cult of Ayn Rand" (1961), he labels Rand "the Joan of Arc of Free Enterprise," while in a flip tone he suggests that her "code of ethics [is] likely to appall even the greediest dollar chaser."[34]

One of the people most upset by Rand's influence on young people is Robert L. White, who as an English professor at the University of Kentucky in the early 1960s found that Rand was the novelist who most impressed his students. White is appalled, not just because he finds Rand "a horrendously bad writer," but because of her ideas, which he finds more horrifying than her writing. In his article "Ayn Rand—Hipster on the Right" (1962), he suggests that her revulsion with "square" society is not unlike that of the "hipster" or the "beatnik."[35] Some twenty years later, Jeff Riggenbach makes a similar contention. In "The Disowned Children of Ayn Rand" (1982), the hippies of the 1960s, but also the militant feminists, gay activists, and pursuers of self-realization of the 1970s are labeled Randians.[36] What both White and Riggenbach contend is that young people read Rand's novels, not her philosophical works, therefore, they interpret her in terms of their own perspectives. White thinks that students, who are in rebellion against their elders and in search of their own identities, associate themselves with Rand's characters who are individuals who do what they think is right and damn the establishment. Riggenbach also notes that Rand's heroic characters are described in youthful images that appealed to those whose watchword was "don't trust anyone over thirty." Although Rand denounced the dominant student movements of the 1960s, calling the students who adhered to them "savages" and "contorted young creatures," she did so in her newsletters and nonfiction works only, and there is no reason to believe that the beatniks, hippies, or other students who "dug" Rand ever read those. Another article that contributes to the overall image of Rand as a strong influence on young people is an interview in *Mademoiselle* magazine, which includes her in their "Disturber of the Peace" series.

While many of Rand's detractors were concerned with the potency of Rand's effect on young people in general, another target for negative criticism was the growing number of Objectivists and students of Objectivism—those people who identified themselves or wished to be identified as followers of Rand's philosophy.[37] Prior to Albert Ellis's *Is Objectivism a Religion?* Nora Sayre's article "The Cult of Ayn Rand" (1966) derided the zealotry of Rand's followers. Sayre calls Rand the "abbess of the acute Right" and satirizes not only Rand but also Nathaniel Branden and the audience members at NBI courses.[38] When this article was republished in her book *Sixties Going on Seventies* (1996), Sayre acknowledged the changing attitudes toward Rand occasioned by the influence of her ideas. Sayre notes: "The first printing of an anthology of her writings, translated into Russian in 1993, sold out in Moscow after two days."[39] Sayre's ridicule of the level of conformity and unquestioning admiration required of Rand's followers predated Jerome Tuccille's more detailed savaging of the smaller meetings of Rand's inner circle. After his break with Rand, Nathaniel Branden, himself the object of much of the satire, joined those who condemned Rand's demands of unswerving loyalty and agreement from her followers. In "Break Free!" an interview published by *Reason* magazine in 1971, Branden acknowledges his role in perpetuating the Ayn Rand mystique and "contributing to that dreadful atmosphere of intellectual repressiveness that pervades the Objectivist movement."[40]

Following up on Sayre's description of the cultish quality of Objectivism, Dora Jane Hamblin's 1967 *Life* magazine article the following year has the same title as Sayre's with the word "angry" inserted to describe Rand. In Hamblin's view, Objectivists are humorless, "ragingly individualistic" adulators of Rand and her philosophy. Hamblin notes the irony of this anticollectivist movement's "almost conspiratorial" Communist cell-like fervor.[41] In the 1990s, Michael Shermer adds his voice to the chorus that calls Rand's followers a cult. He finds this "The Unlikeliest Cult in History" (1993) because it is based in reason.[42] The biggest flaw he deduces in Objectivist reasoning follows from the fact that "morals do not exist in nature and thus cannot be discovered" but must be constructed. When a group sets itself up as the final moral arbiter, it is the "end of tolerance" and ultimately "reason and rationality."[43]

Rand's impact is acknowledged everywhere. A 1961 *Newsweek* article, which generally deprecates her novels, her philosophy, and her followers, compares Rand to Aimee McPherson as a she-messiah who can hypnotize an audience. The article concludes that Rand is "a welcome streak of color in the world of authorship"—a "born eccentric."[44]

In the body of Rand criticism that has been published in general periodicals or newspapers, there are few articles that approach Rand impartially or simply study her ideas in and of themselves. Most essays approach Rand's work from a biographical perspective. Rand as not only author but as public personality looms large over most of the pieces written about her in the 1960s and 1970s.

Rand's works are treated with more equanimity in professional journals. Although academic critics have generally ignored her literary works, there are a few articles about her novels that discuss Rand's books from a pedagogical perspective. In 1966, *Anthem* was included in a *New*

York Times Book Review article about the favorite books of high school students. In 1983, "*Anthem*: A Book for All Reasons" by Tamara Stadnychenko suggests sixteen student projects for either high school or junior college readers of *Anthem* and recommends the book as one that holds the reader's attention and lends itself well to the discussion of fiction's shaping devices, that is, symbols, irony, mythology.[45] My own study in *College English*, "Ayn Rand and Feminism: An Unlikely Alliance" (1978) recommends *Atlas Shrugged* for women's studies courses because of its portrayal of a self-actualized and able adult heroine and a number of its themes that reinforce feminist premises.[46]

"Ayn Rand's Neurotic Personalities of Our Times" (1970) is another of the few articles that deals seriously with Rand as a novelist. Author Paul Deane finds the characters in *The Fountainhead* not only "thoroughly realized" and motivated in a "psychologically valid" manner, but he points out close resemblances between Rand's characters and certain personality types identified by Karen Horney in *The Neurotic Personality of Our Time* (1937).[47] Philip Gordon's "The Extroflective Hero: A Look at Ayn Rand" (1977) uses F. S. Perls's *Ego, Hunger and Aggression* as the basis for a generally negative analysis of the egoism of Rand's heroes.[48] In "Ayn Rand's Promethean Heroes" (1973) John Cody notes the long overdue need to subject Rand's novels to "objective and persuasive literary analysis." Cody's contribution is to trace Rand's self-conscious use of a Promethean sense of life, a vision that proclaims the value of a heroic self-assertion against the established order. Iris Murdoch and Ayn Rand are compared and contrasted in "The Girder and the Trellis" (1973) by Kathleen Collins. Though the Cody and Collins articles bemoan the lack of critical attention to Rand in the established organs of academic criticism, they too are not published in a scholarly journal, but in *Reason* magazine, a Libertarian publication.[49] One wonders if they were submitted to any academic journals.

Attention of the serious academic sort is manifest in two works that contextualize Rand with other important writers of her time. In her chapter on *Atlas Shrugged*, in the anthology *The Other Fifties: Interrogating Mid-century American Icons* (1997), Stacey Olster's generally unfavorable reading compares the withdrawal from society that Rand's heroes choose to similar ideological stances by the protagonists in works of the period by Saul Bellow, Norman Mailer, Ralph Ellison, and Joseph Heller.[50] In "Nabokov, Ayn Rand, and Russian-American Literature" (1995), D. Barton Johnson sees Vladimir Nabokov and Ayn Rand as the "odd couple" of Russian-American literature.[51]

While attention to Rand's literary works is still scant in comparison to that given to her philosophy, she has received some serious notice in social science journals, and as the *zeitgeist* of the times becomes increasingly less hospitable to leftist liberalism, she will probably inspire more consideration. Her anticollectivism and moral defense of capitalism have influenced a number of important politicians outside the United States, including Margaret Thatcher, Malcolm Fraser, and Anders Lange, who headed the Norwegian Party for the Reduction of Taxes and Other Duties and Government Interference. Even Hillary Clinton acknowledges a Rand phase, which Florence King parodies shamelessly as "Hillarique Shrugged" (1994) in *National Review*.[52]

King's jocular tone is also directed toward Rand in *With Charity Toward None: A Fond Look at Misanthropy* (1992).[53] In the chapter, "Our Lady's Juggler Shrugged on the Installment Plan," which also includes some discussion of French novelist Anatole France and Louis-Ferdinand Céline, Rand is labeled "exceptional" and "life-loving," one who disguised her misanthropy as contempt. In King's view, "She carried misanthropy of the naked intellect further than it has ever been carried before or since."[54] King also finds it remarkable that Rand "spent her entire career as a novelist crusading against anti-Semitism while taking care not to write a word about Jews." She hypothesizes that Rand's "whole shtik was a gargantuan displacement of her never-admitted fear of anti-Semitism."[55]

An important study by Norman P. Barry in the *British Journal of Political Science* called "The New Liberalism" (1983), divides Libertarians, or new liberals, and the radical right into two main groups: the consequentialists and the rights theorists. Ayn Rand and Robert Nozick are singled out as the most important "rights" theorists. Murray N. Rothbard's theories are seen as a combination of the two groups. Rand's argument for egoism as a moral doctrine of capitalism and her rejection of altruism are valued not only as original contributions to "rights" theories, but her ideas are seen as catalysts for further innovation in Libertarian thinking, such as in the works of Tibor Machan and Eric Mack.[56]

Rand's works are regularly mentioned in the texts and bibliographies of a number of articles having to do with individual rights, the sociology of thought, journalism, and psychology. In these articles, Rand is cited for her influence on a number of contemporary theorists and as a purveyor of a significant ideology. For example, in his 1996 history of the conservative ascendancy in America, *The World Turned Right Side Up*, Godfrey Hodgson lists *The Fountainhead* as one of "only four books to be counted among the foundation stones of the new conservatism."[57] Norman Barry, in his study *On Classical Liberalism and Libertarianism*, lists Ayn Rand with Friedrich Hayek, Ludwig von Mises, Milton Friedman, Robert Nozick, and Murray Rothbard as "one of many writers who kept the flag of individualism flying during the hey-day of the social democratic and semi-collectivist political and economic consensus."[58] In *Legacy of Wisdom*, John C. Merrill includes her among the great thinkers who influenced journalism. When the focus is economics or business, Rand is also increasingly mentioned. Articles about Alan Greenspan routinely reference Rand's influence, calling her everything from a supply-sider and public-choice economist to an extremely pro-business, right-wing author. Her wide-ranging influence extends to a book on industrial hygiene, which cites her warnings about the effects of egalitarianism in the professions.

Many of the earliest articles about Rand's philosophy appeared in the philosophical journal *Personalist* in the 1970s. In one intellectual interchange, "On the Randian Argument," Robert Nozick's rendition of Rand's argument for property is challenged by Tibor Machan and then by Douglas Den Uyl and Douglas Rasmussen.[59] Machan, in "Nozick and Rand on Property Rights," claims that Nozick paraphrases Rand inaccurately and that actually Nozick and Rand hold the same view.[60] Den Uyl and Rasmussen, in "Nozick on the Randian Argument," also argue that Nozick misstates and misunderstands Rand's position; they offer their own interpretation.[61] Rand's position on property rights is also challenged by George T. Mavrodes, in "Property," who thinks the notion of property rights should be abandoned for the notion of a divisible set of rights.[62]

Rand's name choice for her philosophy and the consistency and integrity of her theories was questioned by a number of writers. In a 1969 article Stephen E. Taylor asked the question, "Is Ayn Rand Really Selfish, or Only Confused?"[63] He finds her moral philosophy inconsistent and its basic tenets unsubstantiated. Kenneth J. Smith analyzes the similarities between Rand's ideas and the principal hypotheses of existentialism in "Ayn Rand: Objectivism or Existentialism" (1970).[64] Prior to Smith's juxtaposing of Objectivism and existentialism, Hazel Barnes devoted a chapter of her book, *An Existentialist Ethics* (1967), to Rand's philosophy, which she terms "Egoistic Humanism."[65] Acknowledging Rand's expressed contempt for existentialism, Barnes still sees much in common between the Rand hero and the existentialist. "[B]oth Objectivism and existentialism call for the assertion of the free individual against those theologies and those oppressively conformist societies which seek to make him deny his unique self in the interests of ready-made social molds and values."[66] Then, Barnes analyzes those areas in which Rand and Sartre agree and those in which they part company. Using Rand's article "Racism" as an example, Barnes points out Rand's questionable reading of history, loose application of terminology, and naive confidence; Rand's attitude toward African American civil rights demands is also seen as an example of her sacrificing certain lesser principles to her most basic principle: "that the government must never interfere with the self-interest of employers or property owners."[67] As a symbol for human aspirations, Barnes finds the dollar sign as unsatisfactory as the cross.

Tibor Machan is among the philosophers who have written most consistently and most positively about Rand. In his editorial introduction to the special Ayn Rand issue of *Reason* (1970), Machan takes exception to those who insult Rand because they disagree with her. While he also disagrees with her on some particulars, Machan believes that Rand is "one of the great geniuses of our time." However, he is not sure she has spent enough time working out crucial areas of her philosophy to ensure her place in the history of philosophy. Machan concludes that she may be remembered as much for her influence on others as for her original works.[68] In "Ayn Rand: A Contemporary Heretic?" (1976), Machan outlines Rand's heretical positions in five areas of philosophy: metaphysics, ethics, epistemology, politics, and esthetics.[69]

Roy A. Childs Jr. is another writer who, although he disagrees with Rand in certain areas, has written positively about her. "An Open Letter to Ayn Rand: Objectivism and the State" (1969) is Childs's invitation to Rand to follow her ideas to what he sees as their logical conclusion and convert to free market anarchism. Childs explains that he thinks Rand is wrong in advocating a limited government; the state is a moral evil that should not be tolerated even in limited form.[70] Childs later changed his mind, convinced that anarchy was "impractical" and therefore misguided. Rand was not convinced by his arguments; Childs's name was removed from *The Objectivist* mailing list. This did not affect Childs's appreciation of her. When Rand died, he called her "a powerful voice for liberty" and wrote about her important contributions to the Libertarian movement in "Ayn Rand and the Libertarian Movement" (1982).[71] Childs lauds her impact: "The point is that no one said it the way Ayn Rand did, with the force of a small but potent nuke."

After Rand's death, *The Objectivist Forum* carried a series of articles assessing Rand's significance in such fields as philosophy, economics, education, psychology, and journalism. These are articles of eulogy, containing neither extended discussion nor proof of her thinking.

One is not quite sure what to make of Claudia Roth Pierpont's 1996 *New Yorker* article "Twilight of the Goddess." The tone is derisive, but the full-page picture and lengthy text are tacit acknowledgment of the significance of the subject. The article is mostly a rehearsal of the plots of Rand's novels.[72] The schism among Rand supporters is the subject of Marci McDonald's "Fighting over Ayn Rand" (1998) in *U.S. News & World Report*.[73] The history of the break between the loyalists at the Ayn Rand Institute and the dissidents forming the Institute for Objectivist Studies is chronicled. It is anticipated that as Rand's ideas gain respectability and her novels become part of the canon, the critical literature will expand accordingly.

REVIEWS

Criticism has had negligible effect on the popularity of Ayn Rand's works. Over the years, there have been those few reviewers who have appreciated not only Rand's writing style, but also her message. Their number is far outweighed by reviewers who have been everything from hysterically hostile to merely uncomprehending. The antagonism of critical reaction grew in direct proportion to the enthusiasm of the reading public.

Rand's first novel *We the Living* did not burst on the literary scene with much fanfare. Lee E. Cannon, reviewing for *The Christian Century* found it "vigorous" and emotionally intense with the characters' motivations clearly drawn, but there is no indication in the composite review, which includes *Norma Darrell* by Beverley R. Tucker and *The Yankee Bodleys* by Naomi Lane Babson, that Cannon found this book, still in print nearly a half-century later, significantly different from the other two, now obscure.[74] Ben Belitt juxtaposes *We the Living* and Alexei Tolsoi's *Darkness and Dawn* as two novels about Russia. Belitt is not convinced that Rand's depiction of the situation in Russia is accurate, but claims he does not want to quarrel with her politics; what he does take exception to is Kira Argounova as a spokesperson. He finds no reason in Kira's actions to respect her judgment; the plot is described as shuttling about "aimlessly from bedroom to rostrum."[75]

One year earlier, the opening of *Night of January 16th* had not been a critical triumph either. Brooks Atkinson, a formidable reviewer for the *New York Times*, found it "routine theatre with the usual brew of hokum."[76] Thirty-eight years later, a revival under the original title *Penthouse Legend* was treated even less hospitably by Clive Barnes. Barnes calls the drama boring and tedious, the writing murky, the acting not particularly good.[77] Walter Pidgeon, however, received good reviews in the original production.

Both sympathetic and hostile reviewers recognize Rand's dramatic power and passionate intensity. The sympathetic reviewers find that these qualities sweep them along; their interest never flags. N. L. Rothman describes the writing in *The Fountainhead* as "strong, dramatic, everywhere intense and highly articulate." He compares it to Sinclair Lewis's *Arrowsmith* in ideals and satiric attack.[78] The *New York Times* reviewer of this novel, Lorine Pruette, characterizes Rand's writing as brilliant, beautiful, and bitter.[79] Like Rothman, she recognizes that *The Fountainhead* is a novel of ideas. Negative reviewers scorn Rand's intensity as overwrought and her drama as melodramatic.

Another recurring criticism of *The Fountainhead* is its length. The *Library Journal* calls it "well written but too long."[80] Diana Trilling calls it "the curiosity of the year" and suggests that anyone who buys it "deserves a stern lecture on paper-rationing."[81] It was published during World War II when many items, including paper, were in short supply. Rand was obviously unconcerned with such fault finding; her next novel, *Atlas Shrugged*, is almost twice as long.

Although the book was enthusiastically received by some important reviewers, the movie of *The Fountainhead* met near universal disapprobation. Released in 1949, some six years after the book's publication, the movie could rely on a presold audience that had ignored the negative criticisms, if indeed they had read them, and put the book on the list of best-sellers. Bosley Crowther disapproves of not only the acting, Patricia Neal's is called "affected" and Gary Cooper's "slightly pathetic," but he also finds the reasoning specious. He cannot understand how Howard Roark's participation in a fraudulent scheme is that much less culpable than that of Peter Keating.[82] Reacting with characteristic derision, *Time's* caustic critic claims that the title of *The Fountainhead* is an understatement; he thinks it should be called a "geyser of emotional sounds and ideological fury." He damns the dialogue, calling it muddleheaded, stagy, and pretentious.[83] Even the usually gentle *Good Housekeeping*, which concedes the importance of Rand's theme, wishes the movie had presented it more entertainingly and with more vitality.[84]

By the time *Atlas Shrugged* was published, Ayn Rand had begun to surround herself with a coterie of admiring readers. Many fans of *The Fountainhead* eagerly awaited the publication of their favorite author's next book. From the fury of the fusillades leveled against it, one might think that an army of detractors was also waiting, lying in ambush. Some of the venom is predictable; Rand's antipathy toward William F. Buckley Jr. and his ilk was well known. Whittaker Chambers lambastes *Atlas Shrugged* in a lengthy article for the *National Review*. Chambers faults the "dictatorial tone," "overriding arrogance," unreprieved "shrillness," and "total absence of any saving humor."[85] With equal fervor and a more vehement vocabulary, the *Atlantic Monthly* reviewer Charles Rolo calls the book "execrable claptrap" and a "solemn grotesquerie."[86] Other reviewers seemed to vie with each other in a contest to devise the cleverest put-downs; *Time* opened its review with "Is it a novel? Is it a nightmare? Is it Superman—in the comic strip or the Nietzschean version?"[87]

Granville Hicks, in the *New York Times*, was put off by what he perceived as the misanthropy that Rand demonstrates in her gleeful destruction of the world. Hicks claims "the book is written out of hate."[88] Helen Beal Woodward's evaluation parallels that of Hicks: "The book is shot through with hatred," writes Woodward, and then lists moralists, mystics, professors, evangelists, Communists, altruists, and bureaucrats as among those that Rand hates. Although Woodward admires Rand's writing abilities—calling her a writer of "dazzling virtuosity"—she feels that Rand wastes her writing gifts by her remorseless hectoring and prolixity.[89]

Atlas Shrugged was not without its critical admirers. John Chamberlain is overwhelmed by the enormity of the task of reviewing such a monumental work. He sees it as a book to satisfy any number of tastes and compares it to Buck Rogers as science fiction, Dostoevsky as a "philosophical detective story," and admires both its "Socratic dialog" and "profound political parable."[90] Richard McLaughlin compares *Atlas Shrugged* to *Uncle Tom's Cabin* in terms of political importance. He is not overfond of Rand's "long-windedness," but he admires her skillful polemics.[91]

After *Atlas Shrugged*, Rand published no more fiction. Although they sell well, none of her nonfiction works approach her fiction in sales. Nor were any of her nonfiction works accorded the same amount of critical attention as *Atlas Shrugged*. Some of the critics of *For the New Intellectual* approved of the idea of gathering all the main philosophical speeches from Rand's novels into one book; others thought it repetitious. Many of the same charges leveled against her novels were repeated against this compilation. Several of the reviews of *The Virtue of Selfishness* point out the similarities between Rand's philosophy and existentialism.[92] Noting that *Capitalism: The Unknown Ideal* is a "melange" from other sources, the *Library Journal* recommends the book be bought only by those libraries in which Rand is in demand.[93] *The Freeman*'s review is appreciative of Rand's "unique arguments" and her explosion of many anticapitalist myths.[94] Honor Tracy titles her review of the same book "Here We Go Gathering Nuts" and compares Rand to those fervent lunatics, in particular the ones who alone knew what was wrong with mankind, that declaimed their views on Speakers' Corner in Hyde Park.[95] Rand's last books of essays, including those published posthumously, received little critical attention except in specialized newsletters and journals.

Renewed attention to Rand's works in both the mass media and scholarly publications was heralded by reviews of the biographical books by Barbara Branden and Nathaniel Branden. *The Passion of Ayn Rand* was reviewed in both *The New York Times Book Review* and the *Times Literary Supplement*. While many of the reviewers expressed negative reactions to the information contained in the book, the work received generally favorable notice. *Judgment Day* also received widespread attention. Subsequently, the *Letters* and *Journals* were widely reviewed. (See Review section of Bibliography for specific citations.)

NOTES

1. Peikoff calls himself an "ideological purist" and is quoted as permitting "no deviations" in Marci McDonald, "Fighting over Ayn Rand," *U.S. News & World Report* (9 March 1998), 54–57.

2. Edward Podritske, executive editor of Second Renaissance Books turned down a request for information about the dates and venues of the audiotapes

offered for sale in his catalog. Dr. Michael Berliner and Scott McConnell have responded to some bibliographic queries, but The Ayn Rand Institute (ARI) turned down a request to do research in its archives. Berliner, executive director, wrote that ARI had not yet faced the issue of opening the archives to independent scholars.

3. Harry Binswanger, editor of the *Lexicon*, states: "I have not used ellipses at the beginning or end of entire passages." He includes square brackets with ellipses in the category of "clutter" (*The Ayn Rand Lexicon: Objectivism from A to Z* [New York: New American Library, 1986], x).

4. The chronology begins with the information that Ayn Rand was "born September 2 in St. Petersburg, Russia." Ayn Rand was born 2 February 1905 (*Letters of Ayn Rand*, ed. Michael S. Berliner [New York: Dutton, 1995], xix).

5. See Chris Sciabarra's review "Bowderlizing [*sic*] Ayn Rand," in *Liberty*, 1 September 1998, 65–66 for details.

6. The character Mr. A, in a comic-book series by Steve Ditko, is derived from Rand's articulation of the philosophical premise that A = A, the title of Part III of *Atlas Shrugged* ("Mr. A," in *The Ditko Collection*, vol. 2, ed. Robin Snyder [Agoura, CA: Fantagraphics Books, 1986], 80–123).

7. The dedication to contemporary rock group Rush's 1976 album *2112* (Canada: Core Music Publishing, Phonogram) reads, "With acknowledgment to the genius of Ayn Rand."

8. In Mary Gaitskill's novel, *Two Girls: Fat and Thin* (New York: Poseidon Press, 1991), she is present, in thinly disguised form, as Anna Granite; in Matt Ruff's *Sewer, Gas & Electric* (New York: Atlantic Monthly Press, 1997), which is dedicated to Rand, she is present in genielike form and has dialogues with one of the main characters. In the campy detective novel *Death Wore a Fabulous New Fragrance* (New York: Berkley Prime Crime, 1998) by Orland Outland, she is referred to as Evgenia Dollars who founded the Church of Dollars, dedicated to the promotion of self-interest. L. Neil Smith's alternative history-science fiction novel *The Probability Broach* (1980) contains mention of Ayn Rand being elected president of the North American Confederacy. In his 1993 novel *Pallas* (New York: TOR), there is a thinly veiled version of Ayn Rand in a character named Mirelle Stein, a writer who publishes individualist anarchist books. One of the chapters is even titled "The Fountainhead." In Gene H. Bell Villader's *The Pianist Who Liked Ayn Rand: A Novella and 13 Stories* (Albuquerque, NM: Amador Press, 1998), the title story is about a young man who unwisely follows Rand's philosophy.

9. Robert Maggio's 1987 *Anthem* trio.

10. "Break Free!" *Reason* (October 1971), 9.

11. Personal interview with Barbara Branden, Los Angeles, CA, 9 November 1981.

12. Albert Ellis, *Is Objectivism a Religion?* (New York: Lyle Stuart, 1968), 70.

13. "Break Free!" 14.

14. William F. O'Neill, *With Charity Toward None* (New York: Philosophical Library, 1971), 14.

15. John W. Robbins, *Answer to Ayn Rand: A Critique of the Philosophy of Objectivism* (Washington, D.C.: Mt. Vernon Publishing Co., 1974), 12.

16. Douglas J. Den Uyl and Douglas B. Rasmussen, eds. *The Philosophical Thought of Ayn Rand* (Urbana and Chicago: University of Illinois Press, 1984), 4.

17. Wallace Matson, "Rand on Concepts," in *The Philosophical Thought of Ayn Rand*, ed. Douglas J. Den Uyl and Douglas B. Rasmussen (Urbana and Chicago: University of Illinois Press, 1984), 19.

18. Barbara Branden, *The Passion of Ayn Rand* (Garden City, NY: Doubleday, 1986), xiii.

19. Virginia L. L. Hamel, *In Defense of Ayn Rand* (Brookline, MA: New Beacon, 1990), 32.

20. Leonard Peikoff, *Objectivism: The Philosophy of Ayn Rand* (New York: Dutton, 1991), xiii.

21. Ibid., xiv.

22. Ronald E. Merrill, *The Ideas of Ayn Rand* (La Salle, IL: Open Court, 1991), 7.

23. Smith's first book, *Atheism: The Case Against God* (Buffalo, NY: Prometheus Books, 1979) is also fully informed by Objectivism.

24. George H. Smith, *Atheism, Ayn Rand, and Other Heresies* (Buffalo, NY: Prometheus Books, 1991), 30–31.

25. John W. Robbins, *Without a Prayer: Ayn Rand and the Close of Her System* (Hobbs, NM: Trinity Foundation, 1997), 23.

26. Ibid., 22.

27. Ibid., xiii.

28. Ibid., 23.

29. Jeff Walker, *The Ayn Rand Cult* (Chicago, IL: Open Court, 1999), 49.

30. Ibid., 2.

31. Nora Ephron, "A Strange Kind of Simplicity," *The New York Times Book Review*, 5 May 1968, 8.

32. Barbara Grizzuti Harrison, "Psyching Out Ayn Rand," *Ms.*, September 1978, 34.

33. Bruce Cook, "Ayn Rand: A Voice in the Wilderness," *The Catholic World*, May 1965, 124. At one point Cook says that the Rand mystique may "prove more attractive than that tired old Norse paganism revived by Paul Joseph Goebbels."

34. John Kobler, "The Curious Cult of Ayn Rand," *The Saturday Evening Post*, 11 November 1961, 98.

35. Robert L. White, "Ayn Rand—Hipster on the Right," *New University Thought*, autumn 1962, 61.

36. Jeff Riggenbach, "The Disowned Children of Ayn Rand," *Reason*, December 1982, 59.

37. Terminology is important in Randian circles. As Rand was extremely zealous about the purity of her ideas and did not want people claiming they were Objectivists when their ideas might differ from hers, she issued "A Statement of Policy" in which she defined Objectivism and delineated the only authentic sources. She then warned against people attempting to act as "spokesmen for Objectivism." Her lawyer Henry Mark Holzer suggested that people who were supporters or interested in learning more about Rand's philosophy should identify themselves as "students of Objectivism." The editor's note in the February 1983 issue of *The Objectivist Forum* states: "The phrase 'students of Objectivism' was originally introduced to avoid implicitly ascribing to Ayn Rand herself the

ideas of her followers and admirers. Now that Miss Rand is no longer alive, this phrase has become unnecessary, and I am dropping it. I will henceforth use the term 'Objectivists' not in an honorific sense but simply to designate those who advocate the philosophy of Objectivism."

38. Nora Sayre, "The Cult of Ayn Rand," *New Statesman*, 11 March 1966, 332.

39. Nora Sayre, *Sixties Going on Seventies* (New Brunswick, NJ: Rutgers University Press, 1996), 177.

40. "Break Free!" 10.

41. Dora Jane Hamblin, "The Cult of Angry Ayn Rand," *Life*, 7 April 1967, 101.

42. Michael Shermer, "The Unlikeliest Cult in History," *Skeptic*, 2, no. 2, 1993, 74–81.

43. Ibid.

44. Leslie Hanscom, "Lecture Circuit: Born Eccentric," *Newsweek*, 27 March 1961, 105.

45. Tamara Stadnychenko, "*Anthem*: A Book for All Reasons," *English Journal*, February 1983, 77.

46. Mimi Gladstein, "Ayn Rand and Feminism: An Unlikely Alliance," *College English*, February 1978, 26. This article is reprinted in *Feminist Interpretations of Ayn Rand* (University Park, PA: Pennsylvania State University Press, 1999).

47. Paul Deane, "Ayn Rand's Neurotic Personalities of Our Times," *Revue des Langues Vivantes*, 36 (1970): 125.

48. Philip Gordon, "The Extroflective Hero: A Look at Ayn Rand," *Journal of Popular Culture*, 10 (spring 1977): 701.

49. Both of these articles, as well as Douglas Den Uyl's "The New Republic," which compares *Atlas Shrugged* to Plato's *Republic*, appear in the November 1973 issue of *Reason*. Another article, not related to Rand's literary works, George Smith's "Atheism and Objectivism" is the fourth article in this special issue dedicated to Ayn Rand.

50. Stacey Olster, "Something Old, Something New, Something Borrowed, Something (Red, White, and) Blue: Ayn Rand's *Atlas Shrugged* and Objectivist Ideology," in *The Other Fifties: Interrogating Midcentury American Icons*, ed. Joel Foreman (Urbana: University of Illinois Press, 1997), 288–306.

51. D. Barton Johnson, "Nabokov, Ayn Rand, and Russian-American Literature: Or, the Odd Couple," *Cycnos*, 12, no. 2, (1995): 102–8.

52. Florence King, "Parodic Verses," *National Review*, 26 September 1994, 61–64.

53. Florence King, *With Charity Toward None: A Fond Look at Misanthropy* (New York: St. Martin's Press, 1992). Inexplicably, King's book bears the same title as an earlier book about Rand, William O'Neill's 1971 publication.

54. Ibid., 124.

55. Ibid., 127.

56. Norman P. Barry, "The New Liberalism," *British Journal of Political Science*, 13 (January 1983): 105–10.

57. Godfrey Hodgson, *The World Turned Right Side Up* (New York: Houghton Mifflin, 1996), 23.

58. Norman Barry, "Ayn Rand and Egoism," in *On Classical Liberalism and Libertarianism* (New York: St. Martin's Press, 1987), ix.

59. Robert Nozick, "On the Randian Argument," *Personalist*, 52 (spring 1971): 282–304.

60. Tibor Machan, "Nozick and Rand on Property Rights," *Personalist*, 58 (April 1977): 192–95.

61. Douglas Den Uyl and Douglas Rasmussen, "Nozick on the Randian Argument," *Personalist*, 59 (April 1978): 184–205.

62. George T. Mavrodes, "Property," *Personalist*, 53 (summer 1972): 245–62.

63. Stephen E. Taylor, "Is Ayn Rand Really Selfish, or Only Confused?" *Journal of Thought*, 4 (January 1969): 12–29.

64. Kenneth Smith, "Ayn Rand: Objectivism or Existentialism," *Religious Humanism*, 4 (winter 1970): 23–28.

65. Hazel Barnes, "Egoistic Humanism: Ayn Rand's Objectivism," in *An Existentialist Ethics* (New York: Alfred E. Knopf, 1967), 124–49.

66. Ibid., 125.

67. Ibid., 141–46.

68. Tibor Machan, "Editorial Introduction: The Significance of Ayn Rand," *Reason*, 7 November 1973, 5.

69. Tibor Machan, "Ayn Rand: A Contemporary Heretic?" *The Occasional Review*, 4 (winter 1976): 133–50.

70. Roy A. Childs Jr., "An Open Letter to Ayn Rand," *Rational Individualist*, August 1969. Reprinted in *Liberty Against Power: Essays by Roy A. Childs Jr.*, ed. Joan Kennedy Taylor (San Francisco: Fox & Wilkes, 1994), 145–56.

71. Roy A. Childs Jr., "Ayn Rand and the Libertarian Movement," *Update on the Libertarian Movement*, April 1982, 4. Reprinted in Childs, *Liberty Against Power*.

72. Claudia Roth Pierpont, "Twilight of the Goddess," *The New Yorker*, 24 July 1996, 70–81.

73. Marci McDonald, "Fighting over Ayn Rand," *U.S. News & World Report*, 9 March 1998, 54–57.

74. Lee E. Cannon, "The Quick and the Dead," *The Christian Century*, 1 July 1936, 941.

75. Ben Belitt, "The Red and the White," *The Nation*, April 1936, 522–24.

76. Brooks Atkinson, review in *New York Times*, 17 September 1935, 26, col. 4.

77. Clive Barnes, " 'Penthouse Legend,' A Courtroom Drama," *New York Times*, 23 February 1973, 20, col. 1.

78. N. L. Rothman, "H. Roark, Architect," *Saturday Review of Literature*, 29 May 1943, 30.

79. Lorine Pruette, "Battle Against Evil," *The New York Times Book Review*, 16 May 1943, 7.

80. Felix E. Hirsch, review in *Library Journal*, 15 April 1943, 328.

81. Diana Trilling, "Fiction in Review," *The Nation*, 12 June 1943, 843.

82. Bosley Crowther, "Gary Cooper Plays an Idealistic Architect in Film Version of 'The Fountainhead,' " *New York Times*, 9 July 1949, 8, col. 5.

83. *Time*, 11 July 1949, 95.

84. *Good Housekeeping*, July 1949, 200.

85. Whittaker Chambers, "Big Sister Is Watching You," *National Review*, 28 December 1957, 596.

86. Charles Rolo, "Comes the Revolution," *Atlantic Monthly*, November 1957, 249.

87. "The Solid-Gold Dollar Sign," *Time*, 14 October 1957, 128.

88. Granville Hicks, "A Parable of Buried Talents," *The New York Times Book Review*, 13 October 1957, 5.

89. Helen Beal Woodward, "Non-Stop Daydream," *Saturday Review*, 12 October 1957, 25.

90. John Chamberlain, "Ayn Rand's Political Parable and Thundering Melodrama," *New York Herald Tribune*, 6 October 1957, sec. 6: 1.

91. Richard McLaughlin, "The Lady Has a Message . . . ," *The American Mercury*, January 1958, 144–46.

92. The reviewer for *Choice* (2 April 1965, 100) says that Rand is "an odd kind of existentialist." Vincent J. Colimore suggests, in his review in *Best Sellers* (1 January 1966, 387), that Rand's philosophy resembles the "[e]xistentialist tenets of Camus, Sartre et al."

93. Jack Van Derhoof, review in *Library Journal*, 1 December 1966, 5984.

94. Elizabeth Gillett, "Other Books," *The Freeman*, 17, no. 3 (March 1967): 189–90.

95. Honor Tracy, "Here We Go Gathering Nuts," *New Republic*, 10 December 1966, 27.

Appendix

What follows is a listing of some works that have been positively reviewed in Objectivist publications. While Rand did not necessarily agree with all the premises of the authors included on this list, she did think enough of these works to have them reviewed in her newsletters and/or to offer them for sale through the Nathaniel Branden Institute Book Service and The Objectivist Book Service.

Abbreviations: The Objectivist Newsletter—ON

                   The Objectivist—O

Anderson, Benjamin M. *Economics and the Public Welfare: Financial and Economic History of the United States, 1914–1946.* ON–May 1965.
Barzun, Jacques. *The American University.* O–November 1968.
Beck, Joan. *How to Raise a Brighter Child.* O–September 1968.
Blanshard, Brand. *Reason and Analysis.* ON–February 1963.
Chu, Valentin. *Ta Ta, Tan Tan.* ON–November 1963.
Crane, Philip M. *The Democrat's Dilemma.* ON–October 1965.
Crocker, George N. *Roosevelt's Road to Russia.* ON–January 1964.
Drury, Allen. *Preserve and Protect.* O–December 1968.
Ekirch, Arthur, Jr. *The Decline of American Liberalism.* ON–July 1962.
Fertig, Lawrence. *Prosperity Through Freedom.* ON–March 1962.
Fleming, Harold. *Ten Thousand Commandments.* ON–April 1962.
Flynn, John T. *The Roosevelt Myth.* ON–December 1962.
Friedan, Betty. *The Feminine Mystique.* ON–July 1963.
Gish, Lillian. *The Movies, Mr. Griffith, and Me.* O–November 1969.
Hacker, Louis M. *The World of Andrew Carnegie.* O–April 1969.
Hainstock, Elizabeth. *Teaching Montessori in the Home.* O–July 1971.
Hazlitt, Henry. *Economics in One Lesson.* ON–February 1962.
Hoffman, Banesh. *The Tyranny of Testing.* ON–March 1964.
Hugo, Victor. *Ninety-Three.* ON–October 1962.
Jones, W. T. *A History of Western Philosophy.* ON–September 1964.

Kaufmann, Walter. *Philosophic Classics*. ON–September 1964.

Keller, Werner. *East Minus West = Zero*. ON–November 1962.

Lyons, Eugene. *Workers' Paradise Lost*. O–January 1968.

Marchenko, Anatoly. *My Testimony*. O–July 1970.

Mason, Lowell B. *The Language of Dissent*. ON–August 1963.

Montessori, Maria. *Dr. Montessori's Own Handbook*. O–July 1970.

Paterson, Isabel. *The God of the Machine*. ON–October 1964.

Randall, John Herman, Jr. *Aristotle*. ON–May 1963.

Scheibla, Shirley. *Poverty Is Where the Money Is*. O–August 1969.

Spillane, Mickey. *The Girl Hunters*. ON–October 1962.

Sutton, Anthony C. *Western Technology and Soviet Economic Development, 1917 to 1930*. O–January 1970.

Toledano, Ralph de. *The Greatest Plot in History*. ON–May 1964.

Von Mises, Ludwig. *The Anti-Capitalist Mentality*. ON–May 1962.

———. *Human Action*, revised edition. ON–September 1963.

———. *Omnipotent Government*. O–August 1970.

———. *Planned Chaos*. ON–January 1962.

———. *Planning for Freedom*. ON–September 1962.

Windelband, Wilhelm. *A History of Philosophy*. ON–September 1964.

Bibliography

What follows is as comprehensive a bibliography on Ayn Rand as has been published to date. A complete bibliography, one that would include all primary and secondary sources written by or about Ayn Rand, is an endeavor worthy of a book of its own. Unfortunately, to date, no one has undertaken such a project. In the meantime, this bibliography should serve both the serious academic researcher and the merely curious reader as a helpful reference resource.

This bibliography, however, is not definitive because *The New Ayn Rand Companion* is designed to be serviceable for the user of the average library. Nevertheless, I have included esoteric sources such as the newsletters of the various Objectivist and Libertarian organizations and institutes that became available to me in the course of my research. Many library reference sources, however, do not index them, and sometimes computer searches will not unearth them. Especially in these days of exploding technologies, libraries often carry a large number of indexes but a limited number of journals or newsletters. Those who wish to explore further will, I am sure, find materials I have missed. There are also sources, such as privately published pamphlets, archival materials, honors theses, discussion papes, lecture notes, pulp magazines, comic books, and articles in pop journals that are not available through normal avenues of library research or in most libraries. Again, I have included such materials as the occasion warranted.

For those interested in exploring beyond the boundaries of library research, there are a number of Internet resources. The World Wide Web abounds with material of all sorts by both serious and dilettante Rand fans. Those interested are encouraged to search the World Wide Web for appropriate websites. A helpful starting point, because of its links to sites that reflect any number of sides of Objectivist issues is The Objectivist Ring [http://www.trail.com/~odysseus/ring/]. Publications such as *Objectivity* and *Full Context* are carried by very few libraries. They are, however, accessible on the Internet, and their home pages include information about the contents of back issues, which can be ordered online. This is true for the more traditional sources also.

Internet discussion groups and news groups devoted to Ayn Rand are another resource. Courses are offered at some sites. One problem with Internet research is the profusion of materials; another problem is reliability and accuracy. There is little, if any, refereeing or reviewing of what gets published on the Internet.

In addition to its comprehensiveness, this bibliography is also the most user friendly to date, organized for maximum research efficiency, separating according to genre, primary and secondary sources, books and articles, reviews and reference entries.

Part I identifies primary sources, that is, the words of Rand, herself. In this section, I have tried to avoid redundancy. Separately published articles or pamphlets that were also published in Objectivist periodicals and later as parts of books are usually not listed separately. While all the publications of Rand's writings to date are included, the listings of speeches and radio and television appearances may not be complete. Neither the Rand estate nor the Ayn Rand Institute have published a complete bibliography to date. Beginning in the 1960s, Rand was a popular lecturer and public figure who made a number of appearances on various talk show programs, such as *The Les Crane Show* and *The Johnny Carson Show*, as well as on a number of college campuses. She was interviewed by Mike Wallace and Edwin Newman, among others. Cataloging all such appearances is beyond the scope of this study, although I have tried to include some of the appearances that are available on video or audiotapes. Second Renaissance Books carries a complete offering of the primary sources and such secondary sources as are philosophically in tune with The Ayn Rand Institute, but their catalog is sorely lacking in information about the dates and context of the audio and videotapes they sell (http://www.rationalmind.com). Laissez Faire Books carries not only primary sources, but also a broad assortment of critical works (http://laissezfaire.org). Principal Source carries material on Objectivism and material of interest to Objectivists (http://ios.org). In the early 1990s, Rand's estate gave some of her papers to the Library of Congress. These consist mostly of various drafts, galleys, and proofs of the novels.

Part II of this bibliography catalogues books, articles, reviews, letters, speeches and other materials written by others about Ayn Rand and her work. In the review section, the reviews are arranged by work to facilitate accessibility. Also included are reviews of the posthumously published edited editions of Ayn Rand's letters, journals, and marginalia. Besides reviews of all the works by Rand, I have provided a sampling of the reviews of the biographical studies. This includes reviews of the biographical documentary *Ayn Rand: A Sense of Life*, which was nominated for an Academy Award for 1997. Review essays appear in the article section. Next in Part II is a section on reference dictionaries, guides, and encyclopedias that contain an entry on Rand or mention her place in contemporary literature. Obituaries are listed with the reference articles. Letters published in response to articles about Rand are listed in the next category. Concluding Part II are the university studies of Ayn Rand. I have included both MA theses and Ph.D. dissertations, but not such studies as senior honors theses. The growing number of university studies testifies to Rand's ingression of the academic community.

The next section of the bibliography, Part III, is composed of representative materials of tangential interest, such as articles or books that are essentially about other matters or individuals but that contain a reference to Ayn Rand. In some cases, this reference is substantial; in others, it is no more than an acknowledgment in a footnote. However, these sources are important in that they help illustrate the extent of her contemporary impact. For those who are interested in Ivar Kreuger, the reporting of whose suicide was the occasion for the writing of *Night of January 16th*, I have included some items about him in Part IV.

PART I: WORKS BY RAND

Books

Anthem. London: Cassell and Company, 1938; revised edition, Los Angeles: Pamphleteers, Inc., 1946; Caldwell, ID: The Caxton Printers, 1953. Paperback: New York: New American Library, 1946. 50th anniversary edition, New York: Dutton, 1995.

Atlas Shrugged. New York: Random House, 1957. Paperback: New York: New American Library, 1957. 35th anniversary edition, New York: Dutton, 1992.

The Ayn Rand Column. Oceanside, CA: Second Renaissance Books, 1991.

The Ayn Rand Reader. Ed. Gary Hull and Leonard Peikoff. New York: Plume, 1999.

Ayn Rand's Marginalia. Ed. Robert Mayhew. New Milford, CT: Second Renaissance Books, 1995.

Capitalism: The Unknown Ideal. New York: New American Library, 1966. Paperback: New York: New American Library, 1967.

The Early Ayn Rand: A Selection from Her Unpublished Fiction. Ed. Leonard Peikoff. New York: New American Library, 1984.

For the New Intellectual. New York: Random House, 1961. Paperback: New York: New American Library, 1961.

The Fountainhead. New York: The Bobbs-Merrill Company, 1943. Paperback: New York: New American Library, 1952. 25th anniversary edition paperback, New York: New American Library, 1971. 50th anniversary edition, New York: The Bobbs-Merrill Company, 1993.

Introduction to Objectivist Epistemology. New York: New American Library, 1979; paperback only. Expanded 2d edition, ed. Harry Binswanger and Leonard Peikoff. New York: Meridian, 1990.

Journals of Ayn Rand. Ed. David Harriman. New York: Dutton, 1997.

Letters of Ayn Rand. Ed. Michael S. Berliner. New York: Dutton, 1995.

The New Left: The Anti-Industrial Revolution. New York: New American Library, 1971; paperback only; revised and expanded 2d edition, 1975. Revised and expanded and republished as *Return of the Primitive: The Anti-Industrial Revolution*, ed. with introduction and additional essays by Peter Schwartz. New York: Meridian, 1999.

Night of January 16th. New York: Longmans, Green, 1936. Paperback: New York: World Publishing Co., 1968, New American Library, 1971.

Philosophy: Who Needs It. New York: The Bobbs-Merrill Company, 1982.

The Romantic Manifesto. New York: The World Publishing Company, 1969. Paperback: New York: New American Library, 1971. Expanded 2d edition, 1975.

Russian Writings on Hollywood. Ed. Michael S. Berliner. Marina Del Ray, CA: Ayn Rand Institute Press, 1999.

The Unconquered (typewritten play manuscript—unpublished). Adaptation of *We the Living*. First New York production, Biltmore Theatre, 13 February 1940.

The Virtue of Selfishness. New York: New American Library, 1964; paperback only.

The Voice of Reason: Essays in Objectivist Thought. Ed. Leonard Peikoff. New York: New American Library, 1988.

We the Living. New York: The Macmillan Company, 1936; London: Cassell, 1937; New York: Random House, 1959. Paperback: New York: New American Library, 1959. 60th anniversary edition, New York: Signet, 1996.

Newsletters

Rand, Ayn, et al. *The Objectivist Newsletter*. Volumes 1–4. New York: The Objectivist, Inc., 1962–65.

———. *The Objectivist*. Volumes 5–10. New York: The Objectivist, Inc., 1966–71.

Rand, Ayn, and Leonard Peikoff. *The Ayn Rand Letter*. Volumes 1–4. New York: The Ayn Rand Letter, Inc., 1971–76.

Articles, Short Stories, Letters

"Ayn Rand Explains." Letter. *New York Times* (11 August 1976): 34, col. 5.

"Ayn Rand Replies to Criticism of Her Film." Letter. *New York Times* (24 July 1949), sec. 2: 4, col. 1.

"The Fascist New Frontier." Pamphlet. New York: The Objectivist, Inc., 1962.

Introduction to *Calumet "K,"* by Merwin-Webster. N.p.: Palo Alto Book Service, 1983. Originally published without the Rand introduction New York: Macmillan, Co., 1901.

Introduction to *The God of the Machine*, by Isabel Patterson. Caldwell, ID: Caxton Printers, 1964; reissued Palo Alto Book Service, 1983. Originally published without the Rand introduction New York: G. P. Putnam's Sons, 1943.

Introduction to *Ninety-Three*, by Victor Hugo, translated by Lowell Bair. New York: Bantam Books, 1962; reissued by Palo Alto Book Service, 1983.

Introduction to *The Ominous Parallels*, by Leonard Peikoff. New York: Stein and Day, 1982.

"J.F.K.—High Class Beatnik?" *Human Events* 17 (1 September 1960): 393–94.

"Let Us Alone!" *Yale Political Magazine* (summer 1964).

"The Money-Making Personality." *Cosmopolitan* (April 1963): 37–41.

"The New Left Represents an Intellectual Vacuum." *The New York Times Magazine* (17 May 1970): 113, 116.

"The Only Path to Tomorrow." *Reader's Digest* 24 (January 1944): 88–90.

Rand, Ayn, Ralph Nader, et al. "Do Our Tax Laws Need a Shake-up?" *Saturday Review of the Society* 55, no. 43 (November 1972): 45–52.

"A Screen Guide for Americans." *Plain Talk* (November 1947): 37–42.

"The Simplest Thing in the World." *The Objectivist* (November 1967): 1–9.

"Textbook of Americanism." *The Vigil* (1946).

"Why I Like Stamp Collecting." *Minkus Stamp Journal* 6, no. 2 (1971): 2–5.

Radio Programs and Television Appearances

"Ayn Rand on Campus." Station WKCR FM, New York, Columbia University, 1 March–17 May 1962.

Ayn Rand—Two Radio Talks. "The Money-Making Personality" and "The Brain Drain." N.p.: n.d. Audiocassette.

"Commentary." Station WBAI–FM, New York, beginning 27 April 1965.

Day at Night with James Day. "Ayn Rand in New York" (videocassette of 1974 appearance on WNET).

Donahue. WGN-TV, Chicago, IL, May 1979 (broadcast from Madison Square Garden, New York).

Donahue. WGN-TV, Chicago, IL, 29 April 1980.

Newman, Raymond. *An Interview with Ayn Rand.* N.p.: n.d. Audiocassette.

Speaking Freely: Edwin Newman Interviews Ayn Rand. N.p.: n.d. Audiocassette.

Tomorrow. Tom Snyder, host. NBC-TV, 2 July 1979.

Wallace, Mike. "Interview with Ayn Rand." *Mike Wallace Show.* 25 February 1959. Videotape.

Translations

These are the translations listed in the National Union Catalog and therefore easily accessible in major libraries.

Atlas Shrugged

Mered ha-nefilim. Tel Aviv: S. Peridamo, n.d.

La Rebelión de Atlas, trans. Julio Fernandez-Yanez. Barcelona: Caralt, 1961.

The Fountainhead

Der ewige Quell, trans. Harry Kahn. Zurich: Morgarten Verlag, 1946.

La Fonte Meravigliosa, trans. Giangi Colombo Taccani and Maria Silvi. Milano: Baldini & Castoldi, n.d.

Ke-ma'yan ha-mitgaber: roman. Tel Aviv: Hotsa'at S. Fridman, 1958.

El Manantial, trans. Luis de Paola. Barcelona: Editorial Planeta, 1966.

La Source Vive, trans. Jane Fillion. Geneva: J. H. Jeheber, 1945.

Night of January 16th

La Nuit du 16 Janvier, trans. Marcel Dubois. Paris: Editions Billaudot, 1946.

The Virtue of Selfishness

Cnota egoizmu. Warszawa: Oficyna Liberalow, 1989.

We the Living

Los Que Vivimos, trans. Fernando Acevedo. Mexico: Editorial Diana, 1965.

Vi, der lever, trans. Else Brudenell-Bruce. Copenhagen: Berlingske forlag, 1946.

Miscellaneous

At the Ford Hall Forum. Talks at Ford Hall Forum, 1961–1981. 17 audiocassettes.

Column. *Los Angeles Times* (weekly from 17 June 1962 to 16 December 1962);

republished as *The Ayn Rand Column* with additional, little-known essays by Ayn Rand. Oceanside, CA: Second Renaissance Books, 1991.

"Conservatism: An Obituary." Speech delivered at Princeton University, 7 December 1960.

"Faith and Force: Destroyers of the Modern World." *Vital Speeches* 26 (1 August 1960): 630–36.

"Fiction Writing." Informal course, 1958. 21 audiocassettes.

"The Forgotten Man of Socialized Medicine: The Doctor." Pamphlet, with Leonard Peikoff. N.p.: 1964.

"From Ayn Rand's Unpublished Writings: Notes for *Atlas Shrugged*," ed. Harry Binswanger. *The Objectivist Forum* (April 1984): 1–8.

"From Ayn Rand's Unpublished Writings: Philosophical Journal," ed. Harry Binswanger. *The Objectivist Forum* (August 1983): 1–8.

"From Ayn Rand's Unpublished Writings: Roark and Cameron," ed. Harry Binswanger. *The Objectivist Forum* (April 1983): 1–10.

"The Sanction of the Victim." Speech delivered at the National Committee on Monetary Reform Conference, New Orleans, LA, 18–22 November 1981. Rand's last public appearance is available on both audio and videotape.

"The Simplest Thing in the World" and "Romantic Literature." Two audio presentations available on a single CD. New Milford, CT: Second Renaissance Books, n.d.

Toffler, Alvin. "*Playboy* Interview: Ayn Rand." *Playboy* (March 1964): 35–43.

Soviet Publications

Rosenbaum, A. *Hollywood: American Movie-City*. Printed without the author's permission. Leningrad: Cinema Printing, 1926.

———. *Pola Negri*. Leningrad and Moscow: Cinematographic Publishing House of the Russian Federation, 1925.

Film

Alessandrini, Goffredo (director). *We the Living*. Adaptation of Ayn Rand novel. Angelika Films, 1942. Originally shown as two separate films: *Noi Vivi* and *Addio Kira*. Italian with English subtitles. Revised version produced by Duncan Scott. Written by Erika Holzer and Duncan Scott.

The Fountainhead. Screenplay by Ayn Rand. 1949.

Love Letters. Screenplay by Ayn Rand. 1945.

You Came Along. Screenplay co-written by Ayn Rand. 1945.

PART II: WORKS ABOUT RAND

Books

Alexander, Jason. *Ayn Rand, Libertarians, and the Fifth Revolution*. San Francisco: Sitnalta Press, 1988.

Amsden, Diana. *An Index to Ayn Rand's "Atlas Shrugged."* Santa Fe, NM: n.p., 1983.

———. *Some Observations on Ayn Rand and Her Work.* North Hollywood: Architekton, 1983.

Baker, James T. *Ayn Rand.* Boston: Twayne Publishers, 1987.

Binswanger, Harry, ed. *The Ayn Rand Lexicon: Objectivism from A to Z.* New York: New American Library, 1986.

Branden, Barbara. *The Passion of Ayn Rand.* Garden City, NY: Doubleday, 1986.

Branden, Barbara, and Nathaniel Branden. *Who Is Ayn Rand?* New York: Random House, 1962; Paperback Library, 1964.

Branden, Nathaniel. *Judgment Day : My Years with Ayn Rand.* Boston: Houghton Mifflin, 1989. Revised and republished as *My Years with Ayn Rand: The Truth Behind the Myth.* San Francisco: Jossey-Bass, 1998.

Den Uyl, Douglas J. *The Fountainhead: An American Novel.* New York: Twayne Publishing. 1999.

Den Uyl, Douglas, and Douglas Rasmussen, eds. *The Philosophic Thought of Ayn Rand.* Chicago: University of Illinois Press, 1984.

Ellis, Albert. *Is Objectivism a Religion?* New York: Lyle Stuart, 1968.

Erickson, Peter. *The Stance of Atlas.* Portland, OR: Herakles Press, 1997.

Gladstein, Mimi Reisel, and Chris Matthew Sciabarra, eds. *Feminist Interpretations of Ayn Rand.* University Park, PA: The Pennsylvania State University Press, 1999.

Hamel, Virginia L. L. *In Defense of Ayn Rand.* Brookline, MA: New Beacon Publications, 1990.

Lepanto, Paul. *Return to Reason.* New York: Exposition Press, 1971.

Machan, Tibor. *Ayn Rand.* New York: Peter Lang, forthcoming.

Merrill, Ronald E. *The Ideas of Ayn Rand.* La Salle, IL: Open Court, 1991.

O'Neill, William. *With Charity Toward None: An Analysis of Ayn Rand's Philosophy.* New York: Philosophical Library, 1971.

Paxton, Michael. *Ayn Rand: A Sense of Life* (a companion book to the feature documentary). Layton, UT: Gibbs Smith, Publisher, 1998.

Peikoff, Leonard. *Objectivism: The Philosophy of Ayn Rand.* New York: Dutton, 1991.

Perinn, Vincent L. *Ayn Rand: First Descriptive Bibliography.* Rockville, MD: Quill & Brush, 1990.

Robbins, John W. *Answer to Ayn Rand: A Critique of the Philosophy of Objectivism.* Washington, D.C.: Mt. Vernon Publishing, 1974.

———. *Without a Prayer: Ayn Rand and the Close of Her System.* Hobbs, NM: The Trinity Foundation, 1997.

Sciabarra, Chris Matthew. *Ayn Rand: The Russian Radical.* University Park, PA: The Pennsylvania State University Press, 1995.

Smith, George H. *Atheism, Ayn Rand, and Other Heresies.* Buffalo, NY: Prometheus Books, 1991.

Snodgrass, Mary Ellen. *Anthem: Ayn Rand.* Jacksonville, IL: Perma-Bound, 1990.

Torres, Louis, and Michelle Marder Kamhi. *What Art Is: The Esthetic Theory of Ayn Rand.* Chicago: Open Court, 1999.

Tuccille, Jerome. *It Usually Begins with Ayn Rand.* New York: Stein and Day, 1972.

Walker, Jeff. *The Ayn Rand Cult.* Chicago: Open Court, 1999.

Articles in Books, Magazines, Journals, Newsletters, and Newspapers

"Atlas Contest Bombs." *Frontlines* 1, no. 8 (April 1979): 1, 5.

" 'Atlas' May Rise Again." *Frontlines* 2, no. 1 (September 1979): 1–2.

" 'Atlas' Rolling." *Frontlines* 1, no. 3 (November 1978): 1.

"Author Wins Royalty Row." *New York Times* (11 February 1936): 19.

"Ayn Rand Reports to S.E.C. Hearings." *New York Times* (9 September 1958): 23, col. 3.

"Ayn Rand Returns." *Look* (14 May 1979): 72–73.

Barnes, Hazel E. "Egoistic Humanism: Ayn Rand's Objectivism." In *An Existentialist Ethics*, 124–49. New York: Alfred A. Knopf, 1967.

Barry, Norman P. "*Ayn Rand and Egoism*." In *On Classical Liberalism and Libertarianism*, 108–31. New York: St. Martin's Press, 1987.

Bear, Mariah. "Fountainhead of Youth." *New York* 26 (31 May 1993): 24.

Berliner, Michael S. "Ayn Rand and Education." *The Objectivist Forum* 3, no. 4 (August 1982): 10–13.

Binswanger, Harry. "Ayn Rand's Philosophic Achievement." *The Objectivist Forum* 3, no. 3 (June 1982): 8–13.

———. "Ayn Rand's Philosophic Achievement, Part II." *The Objectivist Forum* 3, no. 4 (August 1982): 1–3.

———. "Ayn Rand's Philosophic Achievement, Part III." *The Objectivist Forum* 3, no. 5 (October 1982): 1–4.

———. "Ayn Rand's Philosophic Achievement, Part IV." *The Objectivist Forum* 3, no. 6 (December 1982): 1–12.

Bissell, Roger. "Resolving the Government Issue." *Reason* 5, no. 7 (November 1973): 26–29.

Bloom, Allan. "Thoughts on Reading: Ayn Rand, Pop Psychology, and a New Enemy of the Classics." *Chronicle of Higher Education* (6 May 1987): 96.

"Books into Films." *Publisher's Weekly* 136 (30 September 1944): 1418.

Bradford, R. W. "Alan Greenspan—Cultist? The Fascinating Personal History of Mr. Pinstripe." *The American Enterprise* 8 (September/October 1997): 31–33.

———. "Deep Cover Radical for Capitalism?" *Liberty* (November 1997): 37–42.

———. "The Truth and Ayn Rand." *Liberty* 9, no. 5 (May 1996): 39–41.

Branden, Barbara. "Ayn Rand and Her Movement." *Liberty* (January 1990): 49–57, 76.

———. "Passion Play." *Liberty* (July 1998): 29–30.

Branden, Nathaniel. "Thank You Ayn Rand, and Goodbye." *Reason* (May 1978): 58–61.

Brown, David M. "The Critics of Barbara Branden." *Liberty* 1, no. 5 (May 1988): 44–46.

Buechner, M. Northrup. "Ayn Rand and Economics." *The Objectivist Forum* 3, no. 4 (August 1982): 3–9.

"The Chairman's Favorite Author." *Time* (30 September 1974): 87–88.

Childs, R. A., Jr. "Ayn Rand and the Libertarian Movement." In *Liberty Against*

Power: Essays by Roy A. Childs Jr., ed. Joan Kennedy Taylor, 265–81. San Francisco: Fox & Wilkes, 1994.

———. "The Contradiction of Objectivism." *Rampart Journal of Individualist Thought* 4, no. 1 (spring 1968): 84.

———. "Objectivism and the State." In *Liberty Against Power: Essays by Roy A. Childs Jr.*, ed. Joan Kennedy Taylor, 145–56. San Francisco: Fox & Wilkes, 1994.

———. "An Open Letter to Ayn Rand: Objectivism and the State." *Rational Individualist* (August 1969): 145–56.

Cody, John. "Ayn Rand's Promethean Heroes." *Reason* 5, no. 7 (November 1973): 30–35.

Collins, James. "Ayn Rand's Talents for Getting Headlines." *America* 105 (29 July 1961): 569.

Collins, Kathleen. "The Girder and the Trellis." *Reason* 5, no. 7 (November 1973): 13–16.

Cook, Bruce. "Ayn Rand: A Voice in the Wilderness." *Catholic World* 201 (May 1965): 119–24.

Cory, Steven. "Rerouting Ayn Rand's 'Virtue of Selfishness.' " *Christianity Today* 26 (18 June 1982): 72.

"Court Upholds Use of Author's Name in Blurb." *Publisher's Weekly* 195 (31 March 1969): 35.

Cox, Stephen. "Ayn Rand: Theory versus Creative Life." *The Journal of Libertarian Studies* 8, no. 1 (winter 1986): 19–29.

———. "The Films of Ayn Rand." *Liberty* 1, no. 1 (August 1987): 5–10.

Deane, Paul. "Ayn Rand's Neurotic Personalities of Our Times." *Revue des Langues Vivantes* 36 (1970): 125–29.

Den Uyl, Douglas. "The New Republic." *Reason* 5, no. 7 (November 1973): 6–11.

Den Uyl, Douglas, and Douglas Rasmussen. "Nozick on the Randian Argument." *Personalist* 59 (April 1978): 184–205.

"Disturber of the Peace: Ayn Rand." *Mademoiselle* 55 (May 1962): 172–73, 194–96.

Dowd, Maureen. "Where 'Atlas Shrugged' Is Still Read—Forthrightly." *New York Times* (13 September 1987): E5.

"Down With Altruism." *Time* (29 February 1960): 94–95.

Ephron, Nora. "A Strange Kind of Simplicity." *The New York Times Book Review* (5 May 1968): 8+.

Evans, M. Stanton. "The Gospel According to Ayn Rand." *National Review* 19, no. 39 (3 October 1967): 1059–63.

Fletcher, Max E. "Harriet Martineau and Ayn Rand: Economics in the Guise of Fiction." *American Journal of Economics and Sociology* 33, no. 4 (October 1974): 367–79.

———. "A Rejoinder." *American Journal of Economics and Sociology* 35, no. 2 (April 1976): 224.

Forman, Frank. "Ayn Rand and Natural Rights." In *The Metaphysics of Liberty*, 101–12. London: Kluwer Academic Publishers, 1989.

Gimpelvich, Zina. " 'We' and 'I' in Zamyatin's *We* and Rand's *Anthem*." *Germano-Salavica: A Canadian Journal of Germanic and Slavic Comparative and Interdisciplinary Studies* 10, no. 1 (1997): 13–23.

Gladstein, Mimi R. "Ayn Rand and Feminism: An Unlikely Alliance." *College English* 39, no. 6 (February 1978): 25–30.

Gladstein, Mimi R. and Robert Webking. "John Galt's Argument for Human Productivity in *Atlas Shrugged*." *The University of Windsor Review* 21, no. 1 (1988): 73–83.

Goldman, Michael. "Capitalism, Socialism, Objectivism." *Philosophy Research Archives* 12 (1986–87): 143–54.

Gordon, Philip. "The Extroflective Hero: A Look at Ayn Rand." *Journal of Popular Culture* 10, no. 4 (spring 1977): 701–10.

Gotz, Ignacio. "Ayn Rand." In *Conceptions of Happiness*, 417–23. Lanham, MD: University Press of America, 1995.

Greenberg, Paul. "Greed Glorified." In *Resonant Lives, 60 Figures of Consequence*, 150–53. Washington, D.C.: Ethics and Public Policy Center, 1993.

Greenhut, Steven. "Review Raises Brows; Publication Seemed to Fear Any Interest in Ayn Rand or Her Many Books." Editorial/Opinion. *The Arizona Republic* (27 July 1998): B5.

Greenwood, Robert. "Ayn Rand and the Literary Critics." *Reason* (November 1974): 44–50.

Hamblin, Dora Jane. "The Cult of Angry Ayn Rand." *Life* 62, no. 14 (7 April 1967): 92–102.

Hanscom, Leslie. "Lecture Circuit: Born Eccentric." *Newsweek* 57 (27 March 1961): 104–5.

Harrison, Barbara Grizzuti. "Psyching Out Ayn Rand." *Ms.* (September 1978): 24–34.

Haught, James A. "Ayn Rand." In *2000 Years of Disbelief: Famous People with the Courage to Doubt*, 271–72. Amherst, NY: Prometheus Books, 1996.

Heider, Ulrike. "The Queen of Reason: Ayn Rand." In *Anarchism: Left, Right, and Green*, trans. Danny Lewis and Ulrike Bode, 104–7. San Francisco: City Lights Books, 1994.

Houseman, Gerald L. "Ayn Rand: Skyscraper Romance." In *City of the Right: Urban Applications of American Conservative Thought*, 157–84. Westport, CT: Greenwood Press, 1982.

Hunt, Lester H. "In Search of Rand's Roots." *Liberty* 9, no. 4 (March 1996): 51–56. Review essay of *Ayn Rand: The Russian Radical*.

Hunt, Robert. "Science Fiction for the Age of Inflation: Reading *Atlas Shrugged* in the 1980s." In *Coordinates: Placing Science Fiction and Fantasy*, ed. George E. Slusser, Eric S. Rabkin, and Robert Scholes, 80–98. *Alternative Series*, Joseph D. Olander, general editor. Carbondale and Edwardsville: Southern Illinois University Press, 1984.

Johnson, D. Barton. "Nabokov, Ayn Rand, and Russian-American Literature: Or, the Odd Couple." *Cycnos* (1995): 101–8.

Kamhi, Michelle Marder. "Ayn Rand's 'We the Living.' " *Aristos: The Journal of Esthetics* (December 1988): 1–6.

King, Florence. "Our Lady's Juggler Shrugged on the Installment Plan." In *With Charity Toward None: A Fond Look at Misanthropy*, 113–38. New York: St. Martin's Press, 1992.

———. "Parodic Verses: Hillarique Shrugged, after Ayn Rand." *National Review* 46 (26 September 1994): 61–64.

Kobler, John. "The Curious Cult of Ayn Rand." *The Saturday Evening Post* 234 (11 November 1961): 98–101.

Kornstein, Daniel. "Ayn Rand's Legal World." In *The Music of the Laws*, 89–93. New York: Everest House, 1982.

Landrum, Gene M. "Ayn Rand—Macro-oriented Intuitor." In *Profiles of Female Genius*, 299–310. Amherst, NY: Prometheus Books, 1994.

Lennox, James G. "Fletcher's Oblique Attack on Ayn Rand's Economics and Ethics." *American Journal of Economics and Sociology* 35, no. 2 (April 1976): 217–24.

Letwin, William. "A Credo for the Ultras." *The Reporter* 27 (11 October 1962): 56–62.

Lipper, Arthur, III. "Leaders: An Objectivist's Vision." *Venture* 11 (June/July 1989): 18–19.

Locke, Edwin A. "Ayn Rand and Psychology" (part 1). *The Objectivist Forum* (October 1982): 5–8.

———. "Ayn Rand and Psychology" (part 2). *The Objectivist Forum* (December 1982): 12–15.

Macey, Jonathan R. "Ethics, Economics, and Insider Trading: Ayn Rand Meets the Theory of the Firm." *Harvard Journal of Law & Public Policy* 11 (1988): 727–84.

Machan, Tibor R. "Ayn Rand: A Contemporary Heretic?" *The Occasional Review* 4 (winter 1976): 133–49.

———. "Ayn Rand versus Karl Marx." *International Journal of Social Economics* 21, nos. 2–4 (1994): 54–67.

———. "Editorial Introduction: The Significance of Ayn Rand." *Reason* 5, no. 7 (November 1973): 5.

———. "Nozick and Rand on Property Rights." *Personalist* 58 (April 1977): 192–95.

Matzer, Marla. "She the Living." *Los Angeles Magazine* (November 1992): 70–76.

McDonald, Marci. "Fighting over Ayn Rand." *U.S. News & World Report* (9 March 1998): 54–57.

McGann, Kevin. "Ayn Rand and the Stockyard of the Spirit." In *The Modern American Novel and the Movies*, ed. Gerald Peary and Roger Shatzkin, 325–35. New York: Frederick Ungar Publishing Co., 1978.

Merrill, John Calhoun. "Ayn Rand." In *Legacy of Wisdom*, 116–20. Ames: Iowa State University Press, 1994.

Nathan, Paul S. "Books into Films." *Publisher's Weekly* (11 June 1949): 2405.

"NBC Drops 'Atlas.' " *Frontlines* 1, no. 10 (June 1979): 1, 5.

Nichols, Lewis. "Class of '43." *The New York Times Book Review* (22 December 1967): 8.

———. "Talk With Ayn Rand." *The New York Times Book Review* (13 October 1957): 16.

"Note on a Bestseller." *Commonweal* (3 January 1958): 349.

Nozick, Robert. "On the Randian Argument." *Personalist* 52 (spring 1971): 282–304.

Oliver, Charles. "Novelist Ayn Rand: How She Became the Most Influential Writer in America." *Investors Business Daily* (25 June 1998): 1.

Olster, Stacy. "Something Old, Something New, Something Borrowed, Something (Red, White, and) Blue: Ayn Rand's *Atlas Shrugged* and Objectivist Ideology." In *The Other Fifties: Interrogating Midcentury American Icons*, ed. Joel Foreman, 288–306. Urbana: University of Illinois Press, 1997.

O'Neil, Patrick M. "Ayn Rand and the Is–Ought Problem." *Journal of Libertarian Studies* 7, no. 1 (spring 1983): 81–99.

O'Quinn, Kerry. "Ayn Rand's Heroism." *Starlog* 59 (June 1982).

Overbeek, Ross. "Rand-Bashing: Enough Is Enough." *Liberty* 1, no. 6 (July 1988): 56–58.

Peikoff, Leonard. "Ayn Rand." *The Objectivist Forum* 3, no. 3 (June 1982): 1–3.

"People." *Time* (12 January 1976): 32.

Pierpont, Claudia Roth. "Twilight of the Goddess." *The New Yorker* (24 July 1996): 70–81.

Pilpel, Harriet F., and Kenneth P. Norwick. "Can You Name an Author in a Blurb?" *Publisher's Weekly* 195 (5 May 1969): 23–24.

Porter, Kevin J. "Stylistic Considerations for There Is and It Is." *The SECOL Review: Southeastern Conference on Linguistics* 19, no. 2 (fall 1995): 171–83.

Powell, Jim. "Rose Wilder Lane, Isabel Paterson, and Ayn Rand: Three Women Who Inspired the Modern Libertarian Movement." *The Freeman* 46, no. 5 (1 May 1996): 322.

Powers, William. "Ayn Rand Was Wrong." *Washington Post* (25 August 1996): F1, col. 3.

Quito, Emerita. "Ayn Rand." In *Three Women Philosophers*, 36–52. Philippines: National Printing Co., 1986.

Raimondo, Justin. "Who Is Henry Galt?" *Chronicles* (August 1992): 47–50.

"Rand Announces 'Atlas' TV Project." *Frontlines* 4, no. 4 (December 1981): 1, 3.

"Rand Blasts Reaganites." *Frontlines* 3, no. 9 (June 1981): 1.

"Rand Charms Snyder." *Frontlines* 1, no. 12 (August 1979): 3, 6.

"Rand Interviewed." *Frontlines* 2, no. 10 (July 1980): 2.

"Rand on Donahue." *Frontlines* 1, no. 10 (June 1979): 3.

"Reagan's Randians." *Frontlines* 3, no. 3 (November 1980): 2.

Ridpath, John B. "Fletcher's Views of the Novelist's Aesthetic Purpose in Writing." *American Journal of Economics and Sociology* 35, no. 2 (April 1976): 211–17.

Riggenbach, Jeff. "The Disowned Children of Ayn Rand." *Reason* (December 1982): 57–59.

Robinson, Kristin. "Ayn Rand's Objectivism: A Humanistic Interpretation." *The Humanist* (January/February 1989): 29–30.

Rockwell, Llewellyn H., and Jeffrey A. Tucker. "Christian Libertarianism: Ayn Rand Is Dead." *National Review* 42 (28 May 1990): 35–36.

Rothbard, Murray N. "The Sociology of the Ayn Rand Cult" 12 page monograph. Port Townsend: Liberty Publishing, 1987; reprinted Burlingame, CA: Center for Libertarian Studies, 1990.

Rutledge, J. "A Tonic for the Times." *Forbes* (14 September 1992): 556.

Ryerson, Andre. "Capitalism and Selfishness." *Commentary* 82 (December 1986): 37–40.

St. John, Jeffrey. "Are American Students Flunking Capitalism?" *Nation's Business* 55 (July 1967): 90.

St. Paul, F. Blair. "The Randian Argument Reconsidered: A Reply to Charles King." *Reason Papers* 10 (spring 1985): 91–101.

Sayre, Nora. "The Cult of Ayn Rand." *New Statesman* (11 March 1966): 332. Reprinted in *Sixties Going on Seventies*. New Brunswick NJ: Rutgers University Press, 1996 (with "Hindsight" addition: 173–77).

Schwartz, Jerry. "Ayn Rand and Journalism." *The Objectivist Forum* (October 1982): 8–13.

———. "Interview with Ayn Rand." *The Objectivist Forum* 1, no. 3 (June 1980): 1–6.

———. "Interview with Ayn Rand, Part II." *The Objectivist Forum* 1, no. 4 (August 1980): 1–3.

Schroder, Charles Frederick. "Ayn Rand: Far Right Prophetess." *Christian Century* 78 (13 December 1961): 1493–95.

Sciabarra, Chris. "Ayn Rand's Critique of Ideology." *Reason Papers* (spring 1989): 32–44.

———. "A Renaissance in Rand Scholarship." *Reason Papers* 23 (fall 1998): 132–59.

"Second Arbitration on Play Royalties." *New York Times* (17 January 1936): 15.

Shea, Robert. "Ayn Rand Is Still at Work: A Personal Reflection." *Nomos* (May/June 1987): 12–21.

Shermer, Michael. "The Unlikeliest Cult in History." *Skeptic* 2, no. 2 (1993): 74–81. Reprinted in *Why People Believe Weird Things: Psuedoscience, Superstition, and Other Confusions of Our Time*. New York: W. H. Freeman, 1997.

Smith, George. "Atheism and Objectivism." *Reason* 5, no. 7 (November 1973): 18–24.

Smith, Kenneth. "Ayn Rand: Objectivism or Existentialism." *Religious Humanism* 4 (winter 1970): 23–28.

Stadnychenko, Tamara. "*Anthem*: A Book for All Reasons." *English Journal* 72, no. 2 (February 1983): 77–78.

Steele, David Ramsay. "Alice in Wonderland." *Liberty* 1, no. 5 (May 1988): 35–43.

———. "Rand the Primitive" (excerpt from "Alice in Wonderland" by David Ramsay Steele). *Nomos* (May/June 1987): 18–19.

"A Steel House with a Suave Finish." *House and Garden* (August 1949): 54–57.

Taylor, Stephen E. "Is Ayn Rand Really Selfish, or Only Confused?" *Journal of Thought* 4 (January 1969): 12–29.

Teachout, Terry. "The Goddess That Failed." *Commentary* (July 1986): 68–72. Review essay of *The Passion of Ayn Rand*.

"TIA's Interview with Leonard Peikoff." In *The Battle for Laissez-Faire Capitalism*, ed. Peter Schwartz, 56–64. New York: The Intellectual Activist, 1983.

Torres, Louis. "Boswell's Johnson—Branden's Rand." *Aristos: The Journal of Esthetics* (May 1987): 1–6.

Torres, Louis, and Michelle Marder Kamhi. "Ayn Rand's Philosophy of Art." *Aristos: The Journal of Esthetics* (January 1991): 1–5; (September 1991): 1–6; (January 1992): 1–8; (September 1992): 1–8.

Turner, Dan. "Rand Socialist?" *Journal of Philosophical Research* 15 (1989–1990): 351–59.

Veatch, Henry B. "Might 'Objectivism' Ever Become Academically Respectable?" *Liberty* (January 1992): 61–65.

Walker, Jeff. "Was Ayn Rand a Humanist?" *Free Inquiry* (summer 1994): 51–53.

Whissen, Thomas Reed. "The Fountainhead: Ayn Rand (1943)." In *Classic Cult Fiction*, 92–101. Westport, CT: Greenwood Press, 1992.

White, Robert L. "Ayn Rand—Hipster on the Right." *New University Thought* 2 (Autumn 1962): 57–72.

"Who Will Play in 'Atlas': A Frontlines Casting Contest." *Frontlines* 1, no. 5 (January 1979): 6.

Wilson, Colin. "The Works of Ayn Rand." In *The Eagle and the Earwig*, 210–24. London: John Baker, 1965.

Wilson, P. Eddy. "The Fiction of Corporate Scapegoating." *Journal of Business Ethics* (October 1993): 779–84.

Wolcott, James. "Rand Inquisitor." *Vanity Fair* 52 (6 June 1989): 32–38.

Reviews of Rand's Fiction

Anthem

"Briefer Mention." *The Freeman* (21 September 1953): 931.

Atlas Shrugged

Blackman, Ruth Chapin. "Controversial Books by Ayn Rand and Caitlin Thomas." *Christian Science Monitor* (10 October 1957): 13.

"Book Event." *Human Events* 14, no. 43 (1957).

Chamberlain, John. "Ayn Rand's Political Parable and Thundering Melodrama." *New York Herald Tribune* (6 October 1957): sec. 6: 1+.

Chambers, Whittaker. "Big Sister Is Watching You." *National Review* (28 December 1957): 594–96.

Donegan, Patricia. "A Point of View." *Commonweal* 67 (8 November 1957): 155.

Hicks, Granville. "A Parable of Buried Talents." *The New York Times Book Review* (13 October 1957): 4–5.

Hughes, Riley. "Novels Reviewed." *Catholic World* (January 1958): 309.

Malcolm, Donald. "The New Rand Atlas." *The New Yorker* 33 (26 October 1957): 194–96.

McLaughlin, Richard. "The Lady Has a Message. . . ." *The American Mercury* 86 (January 1958): 144–46.

"No Walls Will Fall." *Newsweek* 50 (14 October 1957): 130–32.

Rolo, Charles. "Comes the Revolution." *Atlantic Monthly* (November 1957): 249–50.

"The Solid-Gold Dollar Sign." *Time* (14 October 1957): 128.

Vidal, Gore. "Comment." *Esquire* 56 (July 1961): 24–27.

Woodward, Helen Beal. "Non-Stop Daydream." *Saturday Review* 40 (12 October 1957): 25.

The Fountainhead: The Book

Derleth, August. Review. *Book Week* (13 June 1943): 4.

Hirsch, Felix E. Review. *Library Journal* (15 April 1943): 328.

Pruette, Lorine. "Battle Against Evil." *The New York Times Book Review* (16 May 1943): 7+; reprinted 6 October 1996: 57.

Rothman, N. L. "H. Roark, Architect." *Saturday Review of Literature* (29 May 1943): 30–31.

Trilling, Diana. "Fiction in Review." *The Nation* (12 June 1943): 843.

The Fountainhead: The Film

Crowther, Bosley. "Gary Cooper Plays an Idealistic Architect in Film Version of 'The Fountainhead.'" *New York Times* (9 July 1949): 8, col. 5.

———. "In a Glass House." *New York Times* (17 July 1949): sec. 2: 1.

McCarten, John. Review. *The New Yorker* (16 July 1949): 46–47.

Review. *Good Housekeeping* 129 (July 1949): 200.

Review. *Newsweek* (25 July 1949): 76.

Review. *Time* (11 July 1949): 95.

Ideal

"'Ideal': A Tour de Force from Ayn Rand." *Los Angeles Times* (20 October 1989): F17.

Night of January 16th

Atkinson, Brooks. Review. *New York Times* (17 September 1935): 26, col. 4.

Barnes, Clive. "'Penthouse Legend,' A Courtroom Drama." *New York Times* (23 February 1973): 20, col. 1.

"Blind Jury Finds a Slayer Guilty." *New York Times* (16 December 1935): 22, col. 5.

Garebian, Keith. "*Night of January 16th*: Play Review." *Journal of Canadian Studies* (winter 1987/1988): 137–38.

"Play Uses Audience in Jury Box on Stage." *New York Times* (10 September 1935): 26, col. 1.

The Unconquered

Hartung, Philip T. "The Stage & Screen." *Commonweal* (1 March 1940): 412.

We the Living: The Book

Belitt, Ben. "The Red and the White." *The Nation* (22 April 1936): 522–24.

Bradford, R. W. "We the Revising" (review of 60th anniversary edition). *Liberty* (July 1996): 54–55.

Cannon, Lee E. "The Quick and the Dead." *The Christian Century* (1 July 1936): 941.

Straus, Harold. "Soviet Triangle." *The New York Times Book Review* (19 April 1936): 7.

We the Living: The Film

Bradford, R. W. "Report: The Search for *We the Living*." *Liberty* (November 1988): 17–29.

Cox, Stephen. "Eternity in 2 Hours and 50 Minutes." *Liberty* (November 1988): 30–33.

Kamhi, Michelle Marder. "Ayn Rand's *We the Living*: New Life in a Restored Film Version." *Aristos* 4, no. 4 (1 December 1988): 3–6.

Reviews of Rand's Nonfiction

Ayn Rand's Marginalia

Hospers, John. "Leaving a Margin for Error." *Liberty* (September 1997): 67–68.

Capitalism: The Unknown Ideal

Gillett, Elizabeth. "Other Books." *The Freeman* 17, no. 3 (March 1967): 189–90.
O'Shea, Daniel G. Review. *American* (21 January 1967): 118–20.
Review. *Christian Century* (23 November 1966): 1449.
Tracy, Honor. "Here We Go Gathering Nuts." *New Republic* (10 December 1966): 27–28.
Van Derhoof, Jack. Review. *Library Journal* (1 December 1966): 5984.

For the New Intellectual

Browning, Norma Lee. "Limping Crusade for Intellectualism." *Chicago Sunday Tribune* (19 July 1961): sec. 6: 5.
Caritas, Sister M., C.H.M. Review. *Social Justice Review* (May 1965): 69.
Donahugh, Robert H. Review. *Library Journal* (1 May 1961): 1781.
Hook, Sidney. "Each Man for Himself." *The New York Times Book Review* (9 April 1961): 3, 28.
Review. *The Journal of Family Welfare* 8, no. 1 (1961): 50–51.
Review. *Kirkus Service Reviews* (15 December 1960): 1065–66.
Rosenblum, Joel. "The Ends and Means of Ayn Rand." *The New Republic* 144 (24 April 1961): 28–29.

Introduction to Objectivist Epistemology

Bynagle, Hans. Review. *Library Journal* 104 (1 May 1979): 1062.
O'Neill, William F. Review. *Teaching Philosophy* 3, no. 4 (fall 1980): 511–16.

Journals of Ayn Rand

Brooks, David. "The Wonder That Is Me." *The New York Times Book Review* (5 October 1997): 38.
Sciabarra, Chris. "Bowderlizing [*sic*] Ayn Rand." *Liberty* 12, no. 1 (September 1998): 65–66.

Letters of Ayn Rand

Bradford, R. W. "Rand: Behind the Self-Mythology." *Liberty* 9, no. 1 (September 1995): 51–56.
Cox, Christopher. "Behind *The Fountainhead*." *The New York Times Book Review* (6 August 1995): sec 7: 9.
Frank, Jeffrey A. Review. *Book World* 25, no. 28 (9 July 1995): 4.
Overmyer, J. Review. *Choice* 33 (February 1996): 952.

Sciabarra, Chris Matthew. "Rand the Living." *Reason* 27, no. 6 (November 1995): 52–54.

Winters, Dennis. Review. *Booklist* 91 (1–15 June 1995): 1720.

The Romantic Manifesto: A Philosophy of Literature

Cattani, Richard J. "Ayn Rand and All That." *Christian Science Monitor* (5 February 1970): 11.

Hughes, John W. "None Dare Call It Reason." *The New Leader* (2 March 1970): 21–22.

Michelson, Peter. "Fictive Babble." *New Republic* (21 February 1970): 21–24.

Review. *Kirkus Service Reviews* (15 September 1969): 1049.

Review. *Publisher's Weekly* (6 October 1969): 48.

Review. *Publisher's Weekly* (7 December 1970): 51.

Wadsworth, Carol Eckberg. Review. *The Library Journal* (15 February 1970): 378–79.

Philosophy: Who Needs It

Davis, L. J. "Ayn Rand's Last Shrug." *Washington Post* (12 December 1982): 7.

Den Uyl, Douglas. "Rand's Last Words." *Reason* (May 1983): 71–74.

Svetkey, Benjamin. "The Resurrection of Ayn Rand." *Boston Review* 9, no. 6 (December 1984): 28.

The Virtue of Selfishness

Brodie, Janis M. "Summaries and Comments." *Review of Metaphysics* (June 1967): 729.

Colimore, Vincent J. Review. *Best Sellers* (1 January 1966): 386–87.

Loughan, Thomas. Review. *American* (5 February 1966): 208.

Review. *Choice* 2 (April 1965): 100.

Review. *Kirkus Service Reviews* (October 1965): 1060.

The Voice of Reason: Essays in Objectivist Thought

Raimondo, Justin. "The Voice of Bitterness." *Liberty* 2, no. 5 (May 1989): 49–52.

Reviews of Biographical Works

Ayn Rand: A Sense of Life by Michael Paxton (Documentary Film)

Bradford, R. W. "Making Sense of a Life." *Liberty* (May 1998): 64–65.

Maslin, Janet. "A View of Ayn Rand (with Assistance from the Statue of Liberty)." *New York Times* (13 February 1998): E16.

Sciabarra, Chris. "Ayn Rand: A Sense of Life." *Full Context* (February 1998): 13–14.

Judgment Day: My Years With Ayn Rand by Nathaniel Branden

Brownmiller, Susan. Review. *The New York Times Book Review* (June 1989): 15–16.

Edmonds, Michael. Review. *Library Journal* 114 (July 1989): 78.

Grohskopf, Bernice. "Two Egos." *The American Book Review* (May 1990): 18.
Sobran, Joseph. Review. *National Review* 41 (4 August 1989): 42.

The Passion of Ayn Rand by Barbara Branden

Berger, P. L. Review. *The New York Times Book Review* (July 1986): 13.
Bidinotto, Robert James. Review. *On Principle* (23 June 1986): 6–8.
Chisholm, A. Review. *The Times Literary Supplement* (1987): 893.
Gladstein, Mimi R. Review. *Resources for American Literary Study* 16, nos. 1–2 (1989): 236–40.
Rubin, Merle. Review. *Christian Science Monitor* (29 April 1988): 28.

Reference Articles and Obituaries

American Authors and Books. New York: Crown Publishing, 1962: 603.
American Novelists of Today. Westport, CT: Greenwood Press, 1951: 350.
"Ayn Rand, 'Fountainhead' Author, Dies." *New York Times* (8 March 1982): 6.
"Ayn Rand, R.I.P." *Reason* 14, no. 1 (May 1982): 13.
Bryant, Jerry H. *The Open Decision: The Contemporary American Novel and Its Intellectual Background*. New York: The Free Press, 1970: 169–71.
Buckley, William F., Jr. "On the Right: Ayn Rand RIP." *National Review* (2 April 1982): 380–81.
Cassell's Encyclopedia of World Literature. New York: Morrow & Co., 1973.
"Charles Francis O'Connor, Artist, Husband of the Writer Ayn Rand." *New York Times* (12 November 1979): D11.
Childs, Roy A., Jr. "Ayn Rand 1905–1982." *Inquiry* (26 April 1982): 33–34.
Chira, Susan. "Tributes to Ayn Rand Stress Wide Influence of Her Work." *New York Times* (10 March 1982): 3.
Contemporary Authors, vols. 13–16. Detroit, MI: Gale Research Co., 1975: 654–56.
Contemporary Literary Criticism, vol. 3. Detroit, MI: Gale Research Co., 1975: 423–24.
Contemporary Novelists, 2d ed. New York: St. Martin's Press, 1976: 1139–41.
Gladstein, Mimi. "Ayn Rand." In *American Women Writers: A Critical Reference Guide*, vol. 3, ed. Lina Mainiero, 438–39. New York: Frederick Ungar Publishing Co., 1981. Paperback: vol. 2: 167–68.
———. "Ayn Rand—Sidelights." In *Contemporary Authors: New Revision Series*, vol. 27. Detroit, MI: Gale Research Co., 1989: 395–99.
A Handbook of American Literature. New York: Crane, Russak, & Co., 1975: 407.
Heyl, Jenny A. "Ayn Rand (1905–1982)." In *Contemporary Women Philosophers*, vol. 4, ed. Mary Ellen Waithe, 207–24. Boston: Kluwer Academic, 1995.
"Libertarians Mourn Rand's Death." *Frontlines* 4, no. 7 (April 1982): 1, 3.
McDowell, Edwin. "Ayn Rand: Novelist with a Message." *New York Times* (9 March 1982): 24.
"Obituary Notes." *Publisher's Weekly* 221, no. 12 (19 March 1982): 24.
Oxford Companion to American Literature, 4th ed. New York: Oxford University Press, 1965: 694.
Oxford Companion to Women's Writing in the United States. New York: Oxford University Press, 1995: 739.

Penguin Companion to American Literature. New York: McGraw-Hill, 1971: 213.

Political Profiles: The Eisenhower Years. New York: Facts on File, 1977: 493–94.

The Reader's Encyclopedia of American Literature. New York: T. Y. Crowell, 1962: 937.

The Reader's Encyclopedia of American Literature, 2d ed. New York: T. Y. Crowell, 1968: 840.

Saxon, Wolfgang. "Writer Ayn Rand dies at 77." *Los Angeles Herald Examiner* (7 March 1982): A4, col. 2.

Sciabarra, Chris Matthew. "Ayn Rand." In *Encyclopedia of Ethics.* New York: Garland Publishing, forthcoming.

———. "Ayn Rand 1905–1982." In *American Writers: A Collection of Literary Biographies,* supplement IV, part 2, 517–35. IN: Macmillan, 1996.

———. "Objectivism." In *Encyclopedia of Ethics.* New York: Garland Publishing, forthcoming.

Teachout, Terry. "Farewell, Dagny Taggart." *National Review* 34, no. 9 (14 May 1982): 566–67.

Twentieth Century Authors: First Supplement. New York: Wilson, 1955: 811–12.

200 Contemporary Authors. Detroit, MI: Gale Research Co., 1969: 225–27.

Webster's New World Companion to English and American Literature. New York: World Publishing, 1973: 557–58.

Wheeler, Kathleen M. *A Guide to Twentieth Century Women Novelists.* Cambridge, MA: Blackwell Publishing, 1997: 341.

Who's Who in 20th Century Literature. New York: Holt, Rinehart, 1976: 301.

Writer's Directory. Chicago: St. James Press, 1976–78: 874.

Letters

Branden, Barbara. "In Answer to Ayn Rand." Mailing to subscribers to *The Objectivist* (16 October 1968): 7–12.

Branden, Nathaniel, "In Answer to Ayn Rand." Mailing to subscribers to *The Objectivist* (16 October 1968): 1–6.

———. Letter to the Editor. *U.S. News & World Report* (30 March 1998): BC-15. (Response to Marci McDonald's article "Fighting over Ayn Rand.")

Brandon [*sic*], Barbara, Dorothy Callman, and Alan Greenspan. Letters to the Editor. "Atlas Shrugged." *New York Times* (3 Nov. 1957): sec. 7: 46. (Barbara Branden, Dorothy Callman, and Alan Greenspan remonstrate against Granville Hicks's review of *Atlas Shrugged.*)

Brodsky, Allyn B., et al. Letters to the Editor. "The Rand Phenomenon." *The New York Times Book Review* (9 June 1968): 32. (Nora Ephron's 25th anniversary article on *The Fountainhead* elicited twelve letters.)

Gunkel, Patrick. Letter. "Mr. Reagan's Choice for Vice-President." *New York Times* (1 August 1976): sec. 4: 14, col. 3.

Holton, James E. (archivist, Lewis and Clark College). Letter to Mimi R. Gladstein detailing Rand's visit to that campus, 6 August 1982.

Kelley, David. Letter to the Editor. *U.S. News & World Report* (30 March 1998): BC-15. (Response to Marci McDonald's article "Fighting over Ayn Rand.")

Moffat, Gertrude M. Letter to Editor. *New York Times* (9 October 1935): 22, col. 6.

Peikoff, Leonard. Letter to Editor. "Atlas Shrieked." *Esquire* 56 (October 1961): 14, 20.

―――. Letter to Editor. *U.S. News & World Report* (30 March 1998): BC-15. (Response to Marci McDonald's article "Fighting over Ayn Rand.")

Tracinski, Robert W. Letter to Editor. *U.S. News & World Report* (30 March 1998): BC-15. (Response to Marci McDonald's article "Fighting over Ayn Rand.")

University Studies of Rand

Attarian, John Charles. "Failure of a Vision: Critique of Objectivist Economic Philosophy (volumes I and II) (Ayn Rand)." 45–07A, The University of Michigan, 1984.

Cashill, John Rigers, "The Capitalist as Hero in the American Novel." 43–08A, Purdue University, 1982.

Christian, Juli. "Objectivism Illustrated: Ayn Rand's Integration of Philosophy and Plot in *Atlas Shrugged*." MA thesis. Baylor University, 1985.

Clapper, Thomas Heman. "American Conservative Utopias." 44–02A, The University of Oklahoma, 1983.

Crass, Julianne Elizabeth. "The Tiger and the She-Wolf: The Individualisms of Thomas Hobbes and Ayn Rand." MA thesis. Victoria University of Wellington, 1996.

Cunningham, Lisa Ann. "A Portrait of Media Ethics in the Fiction of Ayn Rand: A Qualitative Analysis." MA thesis. University of South Florida, 1997.

Davisson, Gary. "Ayn Rand's Objectivist Philosophy, Psychology, and Psychotherapy Implications for Therapy." *DAI*, 35-A (June 1975), 7646A, Florida State University.

De Renzo, Denise. "The View from Outside the Prison: Themes of Dominance and Subservience in Ayn Rand's Fiction." MA thesis. Villanova University, 1988.

DeVault, John Henry. "Great and Wise Things: Heroism in the Novels of Ayn Rand." MA thesis. West Virginia University, 1985.

Douthit, Jim. " 'Joanna.' A Two-Act Play in Poetry, Concretizing Objectivism, the Philosophy of Ayn Rand, in the Words and Actions of the Play's Characters." 57–05A, The Union Institute, 1996.

Edgette, Janet Sasson. "Psychoanalytic Application of the Works of Ayn Rand to Adolescence." Psy. D. thesis. Hahnemann University, 1987.

Forman, Frank. "Individualism, Collectivism and Systemism in the Works of Buchanan, Unger, and Bunge (Metaphysics, Liberty, Contractarianism)." 46–04A, George Mason University, 1985.

Girouard, Donna Marie. "An Analysis of Romantic-Realism in Ayn Rand's 'The Fountainhead.' " MA thesis. Florida Atlantic University, 1991.

Hoberek, Andrew Paul. "White-Collar Culture: Work, Organization, and American Fiction, 1943–1959." 59–01A, The University of Chicago, 1998.

Kirell, Leah Rebecca. "Shrugging off Atlas: The Illusion of Individual Autonomy in Ayn Rand." MA thesis. Radford University, 1995.

Lawson, David Clifton. "Ayn Rand: Her Systematic Appraisal of the Problems and Challenges Confronting Modern Man." MA thesis. University of Texas at El Paso, 1969.

Majkut, Paul Theodore. "From Daydream to Nightmare: Utopian Fiction in the Late Nineteenth and Early Twentieth Centuries." 48–03A, Indiana University of Pennsylvania, 1986.

McIlnay, Philip Kent. "Ayn Rand: Objectivism." MA thesis. University of California, Santa Barbara, 1968.

Meyer, Gary B. "The Value of Volition in Ayn Rand's Fiction." MA thesis. Eastern Washington University, 1988.

Mulder, Stacy S. "Objective Romanticism: A Study of the Romantic Roots in the Objectivist Philosophy of Ayn Rand." MA thesis. Ball State University, 1994.

Nighan, Raymond Andrew, Jr. "Ayn Rand's Concept of the Educated Man." DAI, 35-A (August 1974), 859A, Loyola University of Chicago.

Nolan, Karen C. "Ayn Rand and Feminine Consciousness: Liberating the Heroine of the American Novel." MA thesis. Villanova University, 1995.

Osborn, Virginia Jean. "A Critical Examination of the Ethical Philosophy of Ayn Rand." MA thesis. University of Tennessee, 1973.

Parker, Sara Kristin. "Ayn Rand, Female Misogynist: A Study of Androgyny in Atlas Shrugged." MA thesis. Longwood College, 1985.

Pinson, James. "Objective Journalism and Ayn Rand's Philosophy of Objectivism." Ph.D. diss., University of Missouri-Columbia, 1996.

Pitstick, Christina L. "Egoism: The Ethical System of Ayn Rand." MA thesis. Trinity International University, 1997.

Rybinski, Paul. "Frank Norris and Ayn Rand: Contrasting Perspectives." MA thesis. Florida State University, 1993.

Scharf, Uwe C. "Are Objectivism and Christianity Irreconcilable Opposites?" MA thesis. Christian Theological Seminary, 1988.

Sciabarra, Chris Matthew. "Toward a Radical Critique of Utopianism: Dialectics and Dualism in the Works of Friedrich Hayek, Murray Rothbard and Karl Marx." 49–09A, New York University, 1988.

Shamlin, James M. "The Portrayal of the Ideal Man in Ayn Rand's Fiction." MA thesis. East Carolina University, 1993.

Shelton, Scorchy Ray. "Epicurus and Rand: A Comparison of Hedone and Happiness." MA thesis. San Francisco State University, 1995.

Slezak, Sharon Lea. "Fiction and Philosophy: The Novels of Ayn Rand." MA thesis. University of Iowa, 1968.

Snell, Lisa Ann. "The Creation of Historical Reality: An Investigation of Ayn Rand's Social Movement Rhetoric." MA thesis. California State University, 1993.

Stierman, John Phillips. "Ayn Rand and Objectivism: Her Role in American Thought." MA thesis. University of Northern Iowa, 1986.

Stricker, Barry Arthur. "The Life and Thought of Ayn Rand: The Roots of Objectivism." 48–12A, Golden Gate Baptist Theological Seminary, 1987.

Tait, John. "The Rational Egoism of Ayn Rand." MA thesis. Trinity Evangelical Divinity School, 1986.

Vantrease, Brenda Riehman. "The Heroic Ideal: Three Views" (DeFoe, Bronte, Rand). DAI, 41 (1980), 21–06A, Middle Tennessee State University.

Other Materials

Aristos: A Journal of Esthetics (July 1982–September 1997). Ed. Lou Torres and Michelle Kamhi.

Bernstein, Andrew. "The Mind as Hero in *Atlas Shrugged.*" New Milford, CT: Second Renaissance Books, 1994. 2 audiocassettes.

Branden, Barbara. "Ayn Rand: The Charisma of Reason." Speech at Future of Freedom Conference, Long Beach, CA, 23 October 1983.

————. "Who Is Ayn Rand?" Speech at Future of Freedom Conference, Long Beach, CA, 2 October 1982.

Branden, Nathaniel. "The Basic Principles of Objectivism." Audio-Forum. 20 audiocassettes.

————. "The Benefits and Hazards of the Philosophy of Ayn Rand: A Personal Statement." Biocentric Institute, 1982. Audiocassette.

Champagne-Gilbert, Maurice. *The Mysterious Valley*, trans. Bill Bucko. Lafayette, Co: The Atlantean Press, 1994.

Full Context: An International Objectivist Publication 3–11 (September 1990–present). Ed. Karen Minto (formerly Reedstrom). Formerly published as *The Objectivist Club of Eastern Michigan*, 1–2 (October 1988–June 1990).

Gaitskill, Mary. *Two Girls, Fat and Thin*. New York: Poseidon Press, 1991. Novel with Rand-based character, Anna Granite.

Greenberg, Sid. *Ayn Rand and Alienation: The Platonic Idealism of the Objectivist Ethics and a Rational Alternative*. San Francisco: Sid Greenberg, 1977.

The Intellectual Activist 1–9. Ed. Peter Schwartz (October 1979–September 1991); Linda Rearden (November 1991–May 1994); Robert Stubblefield (July 1994–May 1995); Paul Blair (July 1995–September 1996); Robert Tracinski (November 1996–present).

IOS Journal 1–7 (summer 1991–August 1997).

Navigator 1, no. 1 (September 1997). Ed. Roger Donway.

Nichols, Rosalie. *Confessions of a Randian Cultist: An Open Letter to Ayn Rand Regarding the Branden Interview*. N.p.: Brian Eenigenburg Publisher, 1972.

The Objectivist Forum 1–8 (1980–1987). Ed. Harry Binswanger.

Objectivity (Chicago) 1–9 (1990–present). 2 or 3 issues yearly.

Outland, Orland. *Death Wore a Fabulous New Fragrance*. New York: Berkley Prime Crime, 1998. Volume in a campy detective duo series that satirizes Rand as Evgenia Dollars.

Peikoff, Leonard. "Ford Hall Forum Tribute." Introductory remarks, recollections of Rand's final weeks, his delivery of her scheduled lecture. April 1982. Audiocassette.

————. "The Philosophy of Objectivism." N.d. Audiotaped course.

————. "A Study Guide to the Ethics of Objectivism." Pamphlet; revised by Leonard Peikoff and David Kelley. Palo Alto Book Service, 1977.

Plasil, Ellen. *Therapist*. New York: St. Martin's/Marek, 1985. The author's account of her sexual abuse by a therapist recommended by Dr. Allan Blumenthal.

Ruff, Matt. *Sewer, Gas & Electric*. New York: Atlantic Monthly Press, 1997. Futuristic novel with holographic Ayn Rand.

Smith, Kay Nolte. *Romanticism, Rand, & Reservations.* 1990. Audiocassette.

Smith, L. Neil. *Pallas.* New York: TOR, 1993. Science fiction novel in which a main character strongly resembles Ayn Rand.

Sures, Mary Ann, with Harry Binswanger. *Ayn Rand and the Atlas Shrugged Years: Reminiscences and Recollections.* New Milford, CT: Second Renaissance Books, n.d. Audiocassette.

PART III: WORKS THAT REFER TO RAND

Articles and Books that Include References to Rand and Her Ideas

Andelman, David A. "Aggressive Leader for Australia: John Malcolm Fraser." *New York Times* (15 December 1975): 22, col. 4.

Arnoldsen, Larry M. "Reading Made Necessary, Naturally!" *Journal of Reading* 25, no. 6 (March 1982): 538–42.

Axthelm, Pete. "Why It Went Wrong." *Newsweek* (1 November 1982): 38.

Barry, Norman P. "The New Liberalism." *British Journal of Political Science* 13, pt. 1 (January 1983): 99–123.

Beck, Clive. "Utterances Which Incorporate a Value Statement." *American Philosophical Quarterly* 4, no. 4 (October 1967): 291–99.

Binswanger, Harry. "Life-Based Teleology and the Foundation of Ethics." *The Monist* (January 1992): 84–103.

Branden, Nathaniel. "Rational Egoism: A Reply to Professor Emmons." *Personalist* 51 (spring 1970): 196–211.

———. "Rational Egoism: Part II." *Personalist* 51 (summer 1970): 305–14.

"Break Free! An Interview with Nathaniel Branden." *Reason* (October, 1971).

Brownmiller, Susan. *Against Our Will.* New York: Simon and Schuster, 1975: 313–15.

Cerf, Bennett. *At Random.* New York: Random House, 1977: 249–53.

Chamberlain, John. "Edith Efron's Murderous Adding Machine." *National Review* 23 (5 November 1971): 1225–26, 1253.

———. *A Life with the Printed Word.* Chicago: Regnery Gateway, 1982.

Childs, Roy A., Jr. "Professor Kroy on Contract and Freedom: Comment." *Journal of Libertarian Studies* 1 (summer 1977): 215–16.

Den Uyl, Douglas. "Ethical Egoism and Gewirth's PCC." *Personalist* 56 (autumn 1975): 432–47.

Dickinson, Dan. "Dante Plays Prometheus." Review of *Catching Fire* by Kay Nolte Smith. *Reason* 15, no. 3 (July 1983): 64–65.

The Ditko Collection, vol. 2. Ed. Robin Snyder. Agoura, CA: Fantagraphics Books, 1986.

Dwyer, William. "The Argument Against 'An Objective Standard of Value.'" *Personalist* 55 (spring 1974): 165–81.

Ellis, Albert. "Psychotherapy and Atheistic Values: A Response to A. E. Bergin's 'Psychotherapy and Religious Values.'" *Journal of Consulting and Clinical Psychology* 48, no. 5 (1980): 635–39.

———. "Science, Religiosity, and Rational Emotive Psychology." *Psychotherapy: Theory, Research and Practice* 18, no. 2 (summer 1981): 155–58.

Evers, Williamson M. "Social Contract: A Critique." *Journal of Libertarian Studies* 1 (summer 1977): 185–94.

Farnham, Marynia. "The Pen and the Distaff." *The Saturday Review of Literature* (22 February 1947): 7+.

Farr, Finis. *O'Hara: A Biography*. Boston: Little, Brown and Company, 1973: 262–63.

"Film Men Admit Activity by Reds: Hold It Is Foiled." *New York Times* (21 October 1947): 1, 3.

Fitzpatrick, Jerry. *In Defense of Advertising: Arguments from Reason, Ethical Egoism, and Laissez-Faire Capitalism*. Westport, CT: Quorum Books, 1994: xiii, 168.

Forman, Frank. *The Metaphysics of Liberty*. Boston: Kluwer Academic Publishers, 1989.

"Fundamental Fountainhead." *Newsweek* 84 (5 August 1974): 51.

Glennan, Lynda. *Women and Dualism: A Sociology of Knowledge Analysis*. New York: Longman, 1979: 47.

"Goldwater People." *Look* 28 (3 November 1964): 53+.

Haydn, Hiram. *Words and Faces*. New York: Harcourt Brace Jovanovich, 1974: 257–62.

Headlam, Bruce. "Forget Joyce; Bring on Ayn Rand." *New York Times* (30 July 1998): G4.

Hill, Lewis E., and Robert L. Rouse. "The Sociology of Knowledge and the History of Economic Thought." *American Journal of Economics and Sociology* 36, no. 3 (July 1977): 299–309.

Hinchman, Sandra K. "Re-reading Arendt." *Telos* (fall 1993): 164–72.

Hitchens, Christopher. "Downstairs, Upstairs." *New York Times* (1 June 1975): sec. 6: 16–31.

———. "Minority Report." *Nation* (29 March 1993): 402.

Hodgson, Godfrey. *The World Turned Right Side Up*. New York: Houghton Mifflin, 1996: 29–35.

Holland, Thomas P., and Martha A. Cook. "Organizations and Values in Human Services." *Social Service Review* 57, no. 1 (March 1983): 59–77.

Jackson, Robin. *Rational Economics*. New York: Philosophical Library, 1987.

Jelinek, Estelle C. "Anaïs Nin: A Critical Evaluation." In *Feminist Criticism: Essays on Theory, Poetry and Prose*, ed. Cheryl L. Brown and Karen Olson, 317. Metuchen, NJ: The Scarecrow Press, 1978.

Kamm, Henry. "Scandinavia Tightens Hold on Welfare Costs." *New York Times* (22 March 1974): 3.

Katz, Solomon H. "Biocultural Evolution and the Is–Ought Relationship." *Zygon* 15, no. 2 (June 1980): 155–68.

Kelley, David. *The Evidence of the Senses*. Baton Rouge: Louisiana State University Press, 1986: 8, 40–41, 83n, 225n.

———. *A Life of One's Own: Individual Rights and the Welfare State*. Washington, D.C.: Cato Institute, 1998.

———. *Truth and Toleration*. Poughkeepsie, NY: Institute for Objectivist Studies, 1990.

———. *Unrugged Individualism: The Selfish Basis of Benevolence*. Poughkeepsie, NY: Institute for Objectivist Studies, 1996.

King, Billie Jean. "Interview." *Playboy* (1976): 55–70, 194–96.

Kroy, Moshe. "Political Freedom and Its Roots in Metaphysics." *Journal of Libertarian Studies* 1 (summer 1977): 205–13.

Lefevre, Robert. "Professor Nelson on Government." *Personalist* 53 (winter 1972): 74–79.

Lehr, Stan, and Louis Rosetto Jr. "The New Right Credo—Libertarianism." *The New York Times Magazine* (10 January 1971): 24, 86.

Little, Graham R. "Social Models: Blueprints or Processes?" *Impact of Science on Society* 3, no. 4 (1981): 439–47.

Locke, Edwin A. "Critique of Bramel and Friend." *American Psychologist* 37, no. 7 (1982): 858–59.

Lugenbehl, Dale E. "The Argument for an Objective Standard of Value." *Personalist* 55 (spring 1974): 155–64.

Machan, Tibor. *Capitalism and Individualism*. New York: St. Martin's Press, 1990.

———. *Classical Individualism*. New York: Routledge, 1998.

———. "A New Individualist Defense of the Free Market." *International Review of Economics and Ethics* 2 (1987): 27–39.

———. "A Rationale for Human Rights." *Personalist* 52 (spring 1971): 216–35.

———. "Recent Work on Ethical Egoism." *American Philosophical Quarterly* 16 (1979): 1–15.

———. "Some Recent Work in Human Rights Theory." *American Philosophical Quarterly* 17 (April 1980): 103–15.

———. "Why It Appears that Objective Ethical Claims Are Subjective." *Philosophia* 26, nos. 1–4 (1997): 1–23.

———. "Wronging Rights." *Policy Review* 17 (summer 1981): 37–58.

Mavrodes, George T. "Property." *Personalist* 53 (summer 1972): 245–62.

McBride, William Leon. "Philosophy of Law." *Social Research* 47, no. 4 (1980): 775–88.

Miller, Ross. "Burnham, Sullivan, Roark, and the Myth of the Heroic Architect." *Museum Studies* 13, no. 2 (1988): 86–95.

Nealis, Perry M. "Has Neurophysiology Resurrected the Platonic Soul?" *Psychological Reports* 35, no. 1 (1974): 611–19.

Newman, Stephen L. *Liberalism at Wits' End: The Libertarian Revolt Against the Modern State*. Ithaca, NY: Cornell University Press, 1984: 25–30, 94, 112–18, 124, 164.

O'Hara, John. *Selected Letters of John O'Hara*. Ed. Matthew J. Bruccoli, 413. New York: Random House, 1978.

Patai, Daphne. "British and American Utopias by Women (1836–1979): An Annotated Bibliography Part I." *Alternative Futures* 4, nos. 2–3 (1981): 184–206.

———. "When Women Rule: Defamiliarization in the Sex-Role Reversal Utopia." *Extrapolation* 23, no. 1 (1982): 56–69.

Poole, Ross. "Locke and the Bourgeois State." *Political Studies* 28, no. 2 (1980): 222–37.

Rafferty, George. "High School Favorites." *The New York Times Book Review* (27 February 1966): 14, 16.

Rasmussen, Douglas B. "A Critique of Rawls' Theory of Justice." *Personalist* 55 (summer 1974): 303–18.

"The Return of Barbara Branden." *The Smart Set* (February, 1982): 2–4.

Rosen, Gerald R. "Can Alan Greenspan Win?" *Dun's Review* 104 (December 1974): 66–69.

Rush. *2112*. Canada: Core Music Publishing, Phonogram, 1976.

Saint, Andrew. *The Image of the Architect*. New Haven, CT: Yale University Press, 1983.

Schroeter, Rodney. "Ditko: An Overview." *Amazing Heroes* 111 (15 February 1987): 49–53.

Secrest, Meryle. *Frank Lloyd Wright*. New York: Alfred A. Knopf, 1993: 494–98, 510.

Seeger, Murray. "Hope Still Found for Conservatism." *New York Times* (5 November 1964): 20, col. 7.

Smith, George H. *Atheism: The Case Against God*. Buffalo, NY Prometheus Books, 1979.

Spivak, Robert G. "Men Behind Goldwater." *Look* (11 March 1964): 52–59.

Steele, David Ramsay. "Peikoff's Objectivism: An Autopsy." *Liberty* 5, no. 3 (January 1992): 60–61, 66–68.

Taylor, Joan Kennedy. *Reclaiming the Mainstream: Individualist Feminism Rediscovered*. Buffalo: Prometheus Books, 1992: 23–24.

Thorne, F. C. "Essential Man in Society." *Journal of Clinical Psychology* 32, no. 2 (April 1976): 507–8.

Villader, Gene H. Bell. *The Pianist Who Liked Ayn Rand: A Novella and 13 Stories*. Albuquerque, NM: Amador Press, 1998.

Walsh, George. *The Role of Religion in History*. New Brunswick, NJ: Transaction Books, 1998.

Walton, Clarence C. "The Connected Vessels: Economics, Ethics and Society." *Review of Social Economy* 40 no. 3 (December 1982): 251–90.

Wiesen, David L. "Population Obstacle." *Bulletin of the Atomic Scientist* 39, no. 1 (1983): 50–51.

Wilson, Ellen. "Judges, Jurists, and the Legal World of Ayn Rand." Review of *The Music of the Law* by Daniel Kornstein. *Wall Street Journal* (10 March 1983): 26.

PART IV: IVAR KREUGER

Callender, Harold. "Exploring the Kreuger Legend." *The New York Times Magazine* (24 July 1932): 1–2, 13.

"Had Less than $100 on His Arrival Here." *New York Times* (13 March 1932): 22.

"Ivar Kreuger a Suicide." *New York Times* (13 March 1932): 1, 22, col. 8.

"Move to Protect Kreuger Holdings. . . ." *New York Times* (7 May 1932): 23, col. 6.

"Sweden Authorizes Private Moratoria." *New York Times* (13 March 1932): 1, 22.

Index

About the Author

MIMI REISEL GLADSTEIN is Professor of English and Associate Dean of Liberal Arts at the University of Texas at El Paso. In addition to *The Ayn Rand Companion* (Greenwood 1984), she is the author of *The Indestructible Woman in Faulkner, Hemingway, and Steinbeck* (1986) and coeditor of *Feminist Interpretations of Ayn Rand* (1999). She has won international awards for her teaching and scholarship on John Steinbeck.